W9-CPL-934

How Do I Love Thee?

by the same author

BUTTERFLY TAKES COMMAND
BOLD OF HEART
ROYAL GIRLHOODS
THE LOYAL TRAITOR

How Do I Love Thee?

the story of
ELIZABETH BARRETT BROWNING

by *Helen Elmira Waite*

MACRAE SMITH COMPANY
Philadelphia

Library of Congress Catalog Card Number 52–6763

539

TENTH PRINTING

Manufactured in the United States of America

ACKNOWLEDGMENTS

For permission to reprint material copyrighted or otherwise controlled, my thanks are gratefully extended to the following:

HARPER & BROTHERS—for material from *The Letters of Robert Browning and Elizabeth Barrett Barrett, 1845–1846,* Vols. I and II, copyright, 1898, Harper & Brothers; copyright, 1926, Sir Edward A. Altham; and used by permission of the publishers. This material appears on pages 46–7, 52–3, 57–62, 73–4, 83, 98, 101, 105 (from Vol. I); 123, 126, 134–7, 147–8, 162–5 (from Vol. II).

THE MACMILLAN COMPANY—for material from *Letters of Elizabeth Barrett Browning,* edited by Frederick G. Kenyon; copyright, 1897, and used by permission of the publishers.

JOHN MURRAY, LTD.—for material from *From Robert and Elizabeth Browning;* and from *Elizabeth Barrett Browning: Letters to Her Sister,* edited by William Rose Benét, and used by permission of the publishers.

UNITED FEATURE SYNDICATE—for material from *Elizabeth Barrett Browning: Letters to Her Sister,* edited by William Rose Benét, and used by permission of United Feature Syndicate.

TO
Dorothy T. Gray
a token of how I do love her

How Do I Love Thee?

*B*AH!" With the door of 50 Wimpole Street safely shut behind him, Mr. Kenyon felt free to give way to the shudder he had been repressing for the past hour. Even the chilling, smoke-laced January fog seemed more cheery than the company he had just left, he reflected as he groped his way to the hackstand.

"My Cousin Edward," he muttered under his breath, "my Cousin Edward has about as much of a soul as one would find in a lump of suet."

Peering through the curling, brownish London fog, he made out the vague shape of a waiting cab and lifted his voice in a lusty call. A gruff and rather sleepy voice responded, and a moment later Mr. Kenyon hoisted his bulky self into the vehicle with a sigh of relief. Luckily

Cousin Edward and his family dined early. He could reach Lady Margaret Cocks' party at a reasonable hour, and he needed something like the sight of a polka and cheerful talk to take the taste of Cousin Edward Barrett out of his mouth. John Kenyon had a naturally humorous, tolerant, and friendly disposition. He was a person who generally enjoyed everybody, but there were times when he left his cousin's presence feeling positively curdled.

This evening had been an example. From the moment dinner began Mr. Barrett had made it evident that he was displeased with several of his children.

When Arabel asked if Mr. Kenyon had heard that her brothers Stormie and Henry were sailing home from Alexandria, her father observed grimly that they had loitered far too long. If they had been really considerate of his peace of mind they would have turned their faces homeward six months ago rather than run the risk of a stormy winter voyage.

Realizing that this was not the happiest beginning, John Kenyon leaped into the conversation with what should have warmed the Barrett heart—praise of one of his daughters.

"When I came down from Ba's room, I had to pass the music room, and there was Henrietta sitting at the piano, looking so handsome and singing like a bird. Remarkable how her voice has improved."

"Also quite remarkable her choice of an audience." Mr. Barrett looked more and more dour. "I came in early —and what did I see?" The embarrassed Mr. Kenyon watched Henrietta quake under her father's icy look. "I saw Captain Surtees Cook sitting on the sofa, and my daughter was singing 'Love Was Once a Little Boy.' "

So that explained the Barrett mood. A wave of enlightenment swept over John Kenyon. Even he knew that none of the Barrett children would ever be permitted to think of loving anyone besides their father. Furthermore, with the exception of Ba, they were not encouraged to invite their friends to 50 Wimpole Street.

Mr. Kenyon had hastily changed the subject again. "I was quite astounded at Ba's looks this afternoon. She really seemed better and stronger than I've seen her for months. Usually she's very low in the winter."

Arabel turned to him delightedly. "Do you think so too? That's exactly what I've been claiming." But her smile faded as her father drew in his lips more tightly.

"If your sister looks any brighter to you, Arabel, no doubt it is because she is more feverish. We can never hope that she will be more than an invalid needing our tender care. The best we can pray for is that we can make her fading life comfortable."

Alfred and Sette Barrett nodded agreement to this gloomy opinion, but George frowned uncertainly. He played with his glass and then looked at his father and spoke boldly. "Lately I've not been so sure about that. Remember Dr. Chambers' opinion—to get her away from the winter in London—send her to Italy? He said it would be worth all the risk."

Even George, trained lawyer that he was, wilted before his father's scorn. "Do you take me for an inhuman monster, George? Do you think I would consider sending your sister, my darling pet, to die in a strange land? God laid this burden upon her. It is not for us to tamper with His doing. The subject is painful to me. Let us hear no more about it."

Mr. Kenyon squirmed uncomfortably as the cab jolted around a corner. "Bah!" he snorted for the second time. "What a dinner! Good food, perfect servants, handsome lads, and charming daughters around the table—and my Cousin Edward. Sometimes I swear I won't cross his doorstep again."

But there were enchanting, spirited Henrietta, gentle, shy Arabel, and Ba, most of all Ba—all of them much too good for dismal 50 Wimpole Street. He would always go back as long as there was a Barrett daughter in the house.

For Arabel and Henrietta Mr. Kenyon had few fears. Timid and yielding though Arabel was, she was perfectly happy listening to sermons and working for her church, and it seemed reasonably sure that some young curate would eventually persuade her to leave home for his sake. As for impulsive, fun-loving, polka-dancing Henrietta, Mr. Kenyon knew there were two or three young men hovering around her, and he strongly suspected one of them would succeed in carrying her off to a happier life.

But Ba—Mr. Kenyon's heart contracted when he thought of Ba. Most people would have considered her the most fortunate of the three sisters, despite the serious illnesses which had hounded her since she was fifteen. Certainly her sisters and brothers thought her so, because, stern and arbitrary though he was with the rest of them, Mr. Barrett adored, praised, and petted Ba. And she was famous. To her friends and family she might be little "Ba." But to the rest of the world she was Elizabeth Barrett Barrett, one of the outstanding poets of the day.

She might be an invalid, but she had luxuries, love, admiration, a wide circle of friends-by-letter, and a fair amount of fortune—certainly everything that could make "her fading life comfortable." What more could an invalid ask?

She could ask for an abundance of other things, Mr. Kenyon thought. He remembered Ba as he had seen her that afternoon, lying on her sofa, eager, alert, and so intensely interested in everything that her visitor had the sudden conviction she was the most completely alive person at 50 Wimpole Street. She could talk about Benjamin Haydon's paintings, Miss Harriet Martineau's experiments with mesmerism, or the new railroad as readily as she could about her pet spaniel, Flush. When the door of her room closed after him, he had marveled all the way down the two long flights of stairs how anyone could have lain in that one room for nearly four years and still be so quick and keen and delightful.

But with all the affection and care and luxuries which surrounded Ba, something was missing in her room. He had always been baffled to name it, but he had the same feeling in the dining room. Now it flashed over him what it was. There was no hope in the Barrett house. Mr. Barrett would provide his family lavishly with everything else, but they would never know any hope from him.

After the tense dismalness of the Barrett establishment, the atmosphere of Lady Cocks' house was a pleasure. It wasn't so much the brilliance of the prism-hung chandeliers, nor the pleasant hum of conversation, nor even the sight of the gay couples dancing to the lilting music in the ballroom. Certainly there had been sufficient light and warmth at 50 Wimpole Street, but here—John Kenyon found himself expelling a long breath—here people were free to be alive, alive in their own way.

"Oh, Mr. Kenyon!" Mrs. Trollope, a large woman of commanding bearing, evidently had seen him greet Lady Cocks and now was summoning him with an imperious gesture. "So fortunate of you to come! And at just the right moment too. Dear Mr. Browning has been looking for you these last two hours—" She interrupted herself to cast a hasty glance around. "Where is Mr. Browning? Someone tell him Mr. Kenyon has come in."

"Browning is dancing," young Lytton volunteered glumly. "With all the prettiest girls."

"Not all at once?" Mr. Kenyon chuckled, and Mrs. Trollope produced what she considered an arch little smile. "Surely, Ned, you can't hold that against him? And I do confess I wouldn't object to doing a polka or a quadrille with him myself! Well, Mr. Kenyon, if Mr. Browning is dancing, obviously he isn't straining his eyes for a sight of you just now, so do take this seat." The lady indicated the chair beside her.

John Kenyon's eyes strayed wistfully toward the corner where Macready and his friends were gathered. He had intended joining them to hear the news of Macready's latest play, but once Mrs. Trollope laid hold on one—

"As I was remarking, you came at just the right moment." Mrs. Trollope was beaming. "We were exclaiming over Miss Barrett's beautiful poems—so touching they are, only I have never been able to bring myself to read all of 'The Cry of the Children.' It is so affecting! But I simply adore 'Lady Geraldine's Courtship!' Lady Cocks said she thought you were somewhat late because you were at Miss Barrett's. Were you?" Her pause for breath was too short for Mr. Kenyon to do more than nod, and at his confirmation she clasped her hands ecstatically. "Then you did see the dear creature! To think of her writing so bravely while she lies on a bed of suffering. So touching —so romantic!" She reached out and caught the gentleman's sleeve. "Could you do me a great, a tremendous, favor, dear Mr. Kenyon?"

Mr. Kenyon averted his eyes for a second and by doing so met the mirthful gaze of Robert Browning.

"What is your favor, ma'am?" A wholly unnecessary question, for John Kenyon had been asked this favor many times before.

"You are dear Miss Barrett's cousin. Could you—would you arrange an interview for me? I simply must see her and tell her what treasures her poems are."

Inflict this gushing, overpowering woman on dainty, fragile Ba? Not John Kenyon. He withdrew his arm and spoke abruptly.

"I'm sorry, ma'am. It would be impossible. Miss Barrett, I may say, is better than she has been, but anything out of the ordinary is still an ordeal for her. She sees only her family, and a few very close friends. I'm sorry to disappoint you, but if I do not, her father most certainly would."

Now I must ask you to excuse me, ma'am. I see Mr. Horne yonder, and I must speak to him." Mr. Kenyon bowed. "Ah, Browning! I hear you were looking for me? I'm at your service now."

Mr. Browning's blue eyes were still aglint with appreciation as Mr. Kenyon retreated and the two fell in step to cross the room. Mr. Browning had suffered from Mrs. Trollope's rhapsodies over his own poems earlier in the evening.

"Go slow, young man," his companion urged. "You're a famous walker, but I'm a fat old man. Besides my business with Horne will keep until next week if necessary. Our good Mrs. Trollope remarked you had been looking for me for two hours. Tut! Haven't you better ways to entertain yourself at gatherings like this?"

Mr. Browning laughed, showing his very white teeth. And then he flushed, causing Mr. Kenyon to stare at him in amazement. This young man did not have a reputation for being easily embarrassed.

"I—well—oh, the truth is, I have just this week read the two books of Miss Barrett's poetry you so generously sent my sister." Once Robert Browning's tongue was loosed the words poured out in a torrent. "I was in Italy when they were published, you know, and somehow I missed them until now. I'm no Mrs. Trollope, I hope, but Miss Barrett's poetry seems to have gone into me and so become a part of me, and I shan't rest until I've told her so. I had hoped—you took me to call once, before I left for Italy, but Miss Barrett was too ill to see anyone that day— not that I cared too much then—"

Mr. Kenyon's interruption was a little quizzical. "I take it that you would like to call upon Miss Barrett?"

"I had hoped, but then I came up in time to hear your reply to Mrs. Trollope, so I know it's out of the question."

John Kenyon had considered himself perfectly justified in protecting Ba from brazen Mrs. Trollope; but to destroy the likelihood of her knowing Robert Browning— Still, he could not retract the edict which Mr. Browning had just heard him pronounce. And it was true that Ba's visitors saw her only by her own invitation. Here was a situation where one had to move with caution.

"Well, there's always the post, my boy. Miss Barrett is never too ill to read letters—and she does read them, every one."

Browning's face lighted. "And if I tried to tell her what her poetry has done to me, you think she wouldn't be offended?"

Mr. Kenyon's eyes twinkled behind his thick spectacles. "I think I can guarantee that. I'll even venture a prophecy that she'll answer you. And yes, you might indicate that you had hoped for the pleasure of seeing her. It's true enough that she sees no strangers, but—" Mr. Kenyon was speaking earnestly. "I have a fancy you wouldn't remain strangers long."

"I will write tonight," Mr. Browning vowed.

By the time Lady Cocks' guests made their farewells and stepped out into the raw night, the weather had changed for the worse. A fresh east wind was scattering the fog, but an icy rain had begun to fall. Ordinarily Mr. Kenyon, who had a cat's distaste for being wet and cold, would have grumbled in exasperation. Just now, however, he was so thoroughly pleased by his encounter with Robert Browning that he almost ignored the stinging rain.

He was well aware that anyone acquainted with Elizabeth Barrett or with Robert Browning would think he had taken leave of his wits when he urged Browning to bring himself to Miss Barrett's attention. Frail, invalid, sheltered Ba and vigorous, impetuous, handsome, popular man-about-town Robert, who had a reputation for obscure poetry and talked too fast and too loud—what would they ever have to say to each other?

Wholly unreasonable and unlikely, yet Mr. Kenyon had a queer, enveloping conviction that they would have a good deal to say to each other.

And years ago he had decided that Ba might be better if a little life and hope would enter her room. Unfortunately the Barrett doors seemed to be locked against both. His own attempts had met with only feeble success, but with Browning it might be different.

John Kenyon was well pleased with his evening. If he hadn't opened Ba's door, he had at least unlatched it.

*Y*OUNG Ba Barrett herself had once been a small whirlwind of eagerness, ambition, and energy. Even "Bro," her brother Edward who was a year her junior, found her a close match for all his activities.

The Barretts were country children. There were twelve of them; Mary died early, but the others, Ba, Samuel, Bro, Charles John—who was always called "Stormie" because he was born during a thunderstorm—Henry, Alfred, Henrietta, Arabel, George, Octavius, and Septimus, grew up in a queer, Turkish-looking house which Mr. Barrett built in the Malvern Hills. His English neighbors considered it a most peculiar affair, a hodge-podge of domes and minarets, adorned with metal spires and crescents, called Hope End.

There had been a great park to run in or ride through. Ba preferred galloping on her pony Moses, or helping Bro catch lively little field mice and train them as pets, to the proper ladylike pastimes of making ruffled shirts or practicing piano lessons.

Fortunately for her, Mr. Barrett, who for some eccentric reason usually acted as if a parent's duty was to forbid his children doing whatever they really enjoyed, adored her and let her have her own way.

Ba possessed a weapon none of her brothers or sisters could equal. When Mr. Barrett frowned bleakly, little Henrietta or Arabel and even the boys would cower, but Ba would rush to him, seize his coat sleeve and smile enchantingly while she waved a slip of paper before him and cried, "See, Papa! See the poem I've written for you!"

They were good poems too. Mr. Barrett discovered he could be proud of them. He bought Ba little books with silver clasps to use for more poems, which she promptly did, running away from the nursery to hide in her favorite "make-believe house" in the massive sideboard of the stately dining room. At nine she wrote an "epic poem," at ten she produced several tragedies, coaxing her brothers and sisters into acting them, and three years later she was delirious with joy when her father put her first printed poem into her hands. Like authors the world over Ba looked at the title page, glanced hurriedly away, and then her eyes darted back again to make sure the words were actually there.

THE
BATTLE OF MARATHON.
A POEM.
"Behold
What care employs me now,
my vows I pay
To the sweet Muses, teachers
of my youth."
Akenside
BY E. B. BARRETT
London
Printed for W. Lindsell,
87, Wimpole Street, Cavendish Square
1820

Clustering around her, the other Barretts examined the pamphlet with awe. Of course they had seen Ba writing in her little books, and they had spoken the verses she had taught them, but this was printed!

"Just like Mr. Wordsworth's poetry!" Mrs. Barrett exclaimed proudly.

"By E. B. Barrett." Nine-year-old Henrietta followed the words slowly across the page with her finger. "I think that's beautiful."

Little Henry puckered his forehead. "Does E.B. spell 'Ba' just the same as BA does?"

In the midst of the others' laughter his sister hugged him and explained that E.B. stood for Elizabeth Barrett, while ten-year-old George frowned meditatively. Even at ten George was developing symptoms of a pompous air.

"Papa, why didn't you have it say 'By Elizabeth Barrett Barrett'?" he inquired judiciously. "Just E.B. might be Bro."

"No danger!" Young Edward Barrett grinned as he slipped an arm around his sister. "Only one E.B. Barrett writes poetry. Nobody would ever think I've been guilty." But his eyes were alight with pride. Between Ba and Bro was a bond which no one ever shared, and no one surpassed as long as Bro lived.

Mr. Barrett was explaining to George solemnly, "My son, it is not seemly for females to call attention to themselves. Many women who write take some other name as a mask. I am of the opinion your sister deserved to let the world know she wrote this poem, but it would not have been modest for her to flaunt the fact that she is a female."

He drew Ba toward him with the gesture of affection he so rarely used with any of the other children. "But I know what a genius my daughter is, and that's sufficient for Ba, isn't it, my dear?"

Every bright day has at least one bleak cloud, and for Ba the chilling moment was provided by her grandmother, a ramrod of an old lady, who had always viewed her namesake's unorthodox occupations with grim disapproval. Now she looked at her granddaughter's starry eyes with a dour expression.

"I suppose your head will be so turned by your father's nonsense in having this printed that you'll never accomplish anything worth doing again!" she observed caustically. "For my part, miss, I would rather you could show me a neat and proper seam than one line of all the poetry in your pamphlet. Your stitching is a positive disgrace."

Ba flushed, but she was too carefully trained to attempt to defend herself. For once, however, meek and passive

Mary Barrett, who usually sat silent in her mother-in-law's presence, was goaded into a protest. "Any girl can turn a hem! But Mr. Barrett believes, and I agree, that our Ba has a special gift from Providence, and we think she should show it."

The old woman snorted her contempt. "Does she need to show it by untidy seams? Gift of Providence! In my day girls were not gifted by Providence."

A year or so later she snorted again when Ba openly rebelled against the "silly, stupid, bread-and-milk" lessons she had with her governess and pleaded with her father to be allowed to study with Bro and his Italian tutor. Ba was especially fascinated by Bro's stories of Greek history and poetry; but to Mr. Barrett the notion of one of his daughters engaging in something so unfeminine was preposterous. He said No with the sound of a capital N in his voice.

When Henrietta encountered her share of parental refusals she shed a few tears and obediently abandoned her hopes. Even the boys had learned it was wisest to make no appeal and simply swallow defeat. But Ba was of a different caliber. Under her father's pontifical No she was thoughtful, apparently submissive, but she did not wilt.

Two days after he had issued his decree, Mr. Barrett came upon a sight in his rose garden that brought him to a stiff halt. There was Ba in the seclusion of a rose arbor, her dark curls bent eagerly over a book, while another lay beside her on the seat. And both books, unmistakably, were Greek.

"Well, my child, pray what are you reading here?"

The girl started at the suddenness of the stern voice, colored a little, and then smiled confidently into her father's face.

"I am looking into Bro's books, Papa. I know now, after what you said the other day, that it wouldn't be right to waste the signor's time teaching a girl, but I thought perhaps I could pick up a bit here and there by myself." The eager voice dropped to a soft, coaxing note. "All my other tasks are done. You'll let me do it this way, won't you, Papa?"

Mr. Barrett was nonplused. He surveyed the little figure on the arbor seat with a sour expression, and then grim humor lit his eyes, although at the first words of his answer his daughter's heart dropped.

"No, I cannot allow you to study anything so important in such haphazard fashion. Therefore tomorrow report to the signor with your brother. If you must indulge in the study of Greek and mathematics, it is my duty to see you do it regularly and properly."

"Yes, Papa," Ba murmured with demure obedience. But the figure which darted down the garden path ten minutes later would hardly have been called demure, and her grandmother certainly would not have approved the breathless, exultant report Ba gave Bro when she found him.

The Italian tutor sighed and shrugged at the thought of a girl pupil. The little one wrote verses, yes. Her father thought her gifted, naturally, but to keep pace with the subjects he taught her brother— He shrugged again. By the end of the first fortnight he was interested, then amazed, and before he had taught her six months, he was eagerly enthusiastic. *"Testa lunga,"* headlong spirit, he called her. Mathematics never penetrated Ba's brain, but she raced along in her other subjects, and once she touched Greek she threw aside all rules and lexicons and plunged into the strange difficult passages in a way few of the boys he had prepared for universities would have equaled. To Ba Greek was not a lesson—it was music and glory and beauty, and she never had enough of it. She loved it all her life.

Headlong spirit was a good name for this tempestuous, ambitious, impatient, eager girl.

Tragically enough, this headlong quality led her into a serious accident when she was fifteen. One day, when she and Bro were ready for their ride, neither her black pony Moses nor the groom who cared for him was in evidence. Bro was already mounted and making teasing threats to be off.

"I could be by now halfway to the park, instead of waiting for that stupid Dawson! I've a good mind to shake you and Moses altogether this morning."

His sister never heard the end of that sentence. She was racing toward the stables, calling with breathless impatience, "Dawson! *Dawson!"*

When she reached the stables there was still no sign of the negligent groom, nor did anyone else happen to be about. Ba stamped her foot impatiently, and then, fearful of keeping her brother waiting, led Moses from his stall and began to saddle him herself. The saddle was heavier than she had anticipated. Tightening the girth was an exertion which made her delicate fingers burn and brought a swift, startling pain across her back, but by the time Bro came to investigate she was laughing and eager to show what she had done for herself.

That was the last wild gallop Ba Barrett was destined to have. Before they had covered half a mile she almost collapsed with pain, and only some miracle of her indomitable will held her in the saddle while her terrified brother slowly led the pony home.

$\mathcal{T}$HE accident with the saddle seemed to mark the beginning of gathering clouds in Elizabeth Barrett's sky. Hitherto her days had been sunny with good fortune, love and admiration, and keen joy. Now they were filled with exactly the opposite.

Not that the saddle injury was permanent. The strain itself was cured by a few months' rest in bed, and the only reminder Ba had afterward was a slight forward thrust of the shoulders. Something had happened, however, which left her too easy a prey for every other ill wind. Although she was always of a delicate frame, her active, out-of-door life had kept her brimming with health. Perhaps the months of being bedridden and shut-in robbed her of her vitality, for now she apparently had no resistance to the pleurisy which attacked her so severely that it permanently damaged one lung.

When Ba was twenty-one, gentle Mary Barrett died. Subsequently Mr. Barrett decided to sell Hope End, and after a few years in Sidmouth proceeded in 1835 to take his family to London.

Most of the Barretts liked the idea. None of them had ever had much chance to see anything or know anyone away from the distinctly lonely Hope End. Henrietta especially was thrilled.

"Only think, Ba! There'll be parties and dancing—"

"And there will be poets in London for you to meet, Ba," added the considerate Arabel.

"Poets who will come to admire Miss Barrett and stay to marvel at her combination of superior gifts and charm," supplemented Bro. But for all the banter in his voice there was deep affection too, and strong pride lit his face. "You'll be the lioness of London, Ba, and I'll be proud to be your escort."

Ba laughed and flushed a little. Tucked in an out-of-the-way corner of England, she could only dream of meeting the people whose books excited and awed her. But perhaps in London—Papa's cousin, Mr. John Kenyon, who evidently knew everybody in London, had written that he was looking forward to presenting Ba to his friends, Walter Savage Landor, old Mr. Wordsworth, and Miss Mary Russell Mitford. Ba shivered a little but she was thrilled too.

But there were evils in London as well as poets. A disastrous amount of fog and smoke and a raw climate almost succeeded in killing Ba. She had been fragile at Hope End. But after two or three fairly active years in London she became desperately ill. Two specialists came, made their report to Dr. Chambers, and went away again. Dr. Chambers squared his shoulders and turned to Henrietta, who was watching him with pleading eyes.

"Miss Henrietta, I must consult with your father at once."

Henrietta swallowed, nodded, managed to whisper, "Yes, s-sir," under her breath, led the way to her father's study, and then hurriedly retreated.

None of the Barretts was a deliberate eavesdropper, but the rumble of voices in the study grew louder and more ominous. Arabel and Henrietta clutched each other and Bro paced grimly up and down the drawing room until the study door was hurled open and Dr. Chambers flung himself into the hall. He was violently angry, and the Barretts needed only one glance at their father's cold face to know he was in what was called "Papa's displeasure."

"Very well, sir! You have had fair warning with three opinions!" Dr. Chambers was exclaiming as he reached the entrance door. "Flout us if you will, but the results will be upon your own head."

Mr. Barrett bowed stiffly. "I will accept them sir. I still believe a father knows best for his children." He closed the door upon the departing physician and swung about to face the fearful trio with scorching eyes.

"So—my children turn eavesdroppers?"

Arabel gave a quick sob, Henrietta cowered, Edward

colored angrily and spoke heatedly. "No, sir! We did not understand one word. But we are anxious—"

His father favored him with a look of complete scorn. "Anxious—hah!" He repeated the word bitterly, then strode away and locked himself inside his study.

Several days later he informed the family that Dr. Chambers and the two specialists had agreed Ba could not survive another winter in London. The only chance for her, according to them, would be a year in a mild, sunny climate. They had suggested Italy. Which was impossible, since Mr. Barrett could not leave England.

"Let me take her, sir!" Bro cried eagerly. "I will give her every care. Arabel can go with us."

Mr. Barrett surveyed his son icily. "Have I not said I cannot go? And so your sister does not go. What can you be thinking of—that I would send my darling away from me to die?"

"I am thinking of Ba, sir. If this should be her only chance—"

To have his eldest son, now a full-grown man, face him with such a purposeful air set Mr. Barrett back in his chair aghast and speechless. And then his wrath broke through. "To think of one of my sons being guilty of such preposterous impertinence. Leave the room, sir."

Young Edward left, and although it was obvious that Ba grew more ill each day, no one ventured to mention the doctors' ultimatum.

At length Mr. Barrett did vouchsafe the news Ba was to be moved to Torquay, a little seaside town where the winters were mild, and where the Barretts had an aunt who would oversee Ba's care. Arabel would be with her, and so would Bro, at least until everything was safely established.

Torquay failed to work a miracle; Ba was better, but weak and nervous. She clung to her brother, and Edward willingly stayed with her, month after month. A second winter came and went. Ba and Arabel and Bro had been in Torquay fourteen months. Much too long for a young man to idle away his time at a small seaside resort, Mr. Barrett decided. He summoned Bro to London. He had made plans for this eldest son to go to Jamaica to look after the family estates. The thought of Bro leaving her brought on a relapse for Ba. She clung to her brother and could not let him go.

"Write to your father," commanded Aunt Jane Hedley. "Tell him Edward must not leave Ba on any account."

But Arabel only shrank and quivered. "I wouldn't dare!" she confessed. And Bro shook his head.

"He would only order me home by the next post."

Aunt Jane surveyed her niece and nephew with astonishment. Then her mouth tightened. She stood up, shook down her ruffles, and announced crisply, "Then I shall take matters into my own hands. Your father will hear from me, I can promise you! But first I must go talk to that poor lamb upstairs."

Lying miserable and shaken on the bed, Ba was suddenly aware that Aunt Jane had come into the room like a fresh sea breeze. She knew exactly how to cross a sick-

room, did Aunt Jane, neither with stealth nor with too
heavy a tread. She looked down at the forlorn Ba and
before she said a word she brought a fresh cool pillow to
replace the hot, tumbled one under Ba's head. Then she
was smoothing out the tangled curls and kissing away the
tears. "Stop wasting your strength in tears, my lamb.
Stormie or George can go to Jamaica perfectly well. I am
on my way to write your father a letter. I intend to tell
him that Edward is the best medicine you can have, and
that if he is called away from you, your heart will break.
And I do not propose having your heart broken while you
are under my care!"

To think of anyone writing so to Papa! Ba gasped at the
rashness. And when the next post brought her father's
answer she gasped again, this time under the sting of his
words.

"Under such circumstances I do not refuse to suspend
my purpose, but I consider it *very wrong of my daughter
to exact such a thing!*"

Ba cringed at the words, but Bro read them with a
curious smile.

"It wouldn't have mattered whatever Papa's answer
had been, Ba," Edward said as he folded the letter. The
sound of his voice surprised her, it was so deep and
strong. "I have been reorganizing my ideas and my life
these past few days. From now on I'm going to behave
like a man. And I tell you truly, I love you better than
anyone else, and I will not leave you. I will stay by you
until you are well."

She hid her face on his sleeve. "Oh, Bro, if you only could! But it will displease dear Papa so—"

"From now on I am bound to please *you*," he promised her.

But ten days afterward he had left her with finality.

It was a glorious, hot, sunny Saturday in July, and Bro told her in the morning that he was going for a day's sail with Captain Carlyle Clarke and Charles Vannek in the captain's sturdy little yacht. They would be back before dusk.

Ba lay and watched him leap down the beach outside her windows and had a sudden surging longing to go with him, to feel the touch of salt air on her lips and the light breeze through her hair. At that minute she would have given all the poetry she had ever written to be strong and free and to have gone aboard the *Belle* with her brother.

Just how many hours passed when a vague frightened feeling took possession of her, she didn't know. It was absurd; she had no reason for it. There was no cloud in the sky, but the feeling persisted, stronger and more insistent until it nearly choked her. She did not dare tell Arabel, but she beat her hands together and prayed for dusk to come, dusk—and Bro, so that she could tell him about her foolishness and they could laugh it away together.

Dusk came, and then night, but no sound of familiar, running steps, no laughing voice, eager to tell the adventures of the day. Arabel and Aunt Jane assured Ba over and over again of the peacefulness of the star-

crowded night, and she could hear the gentle lap-lap murmuring of the little waves as they touched shore. No, no,
nothing could have happened! There'd been no storm.
The *Belle* was a fleet, sturdy yacht, and the three young
men were all experienced sailors.

But there was no beating down the rising feeling of im-
pending doom. Ba fought against it, but it came stronger
and stronger, bringing a salty taste in her mouth and a
knife of pain with every throb of her heart.

"Come, Ba, love," Aunt Jane spoke cheerily as she
offered Ba her nightly potion. "Take your medicine and
get some sleep so you will be fresh and bright to greet
Bro in the morning. I am certain that the young scamps
made too long a run to turn back this afternoon and that
they'll be coming in with the dawn. Edward will be here
when you wake, I promise you, my lamb."

Somehow Ba's lips managed to curve in a stiff smile.
Surely Aunt Jane must be right! This awful premonition
was only a trick of her nerves. At any rate, she mustn't
keep Aunt Jane here all night. Obediently she took the
medicine. And surely—oh, God was good. He would
grant that her eyes would rest on her brother's face when
she woke.

But it was only Arabel who was beside her in the morning, an Arabel whose cheeks were white and tear-stained.
Ba's throat was suddenly so constricted that no sound
emerged from her moving lips. Only her pleading eyes
asked her desperate question.

With a strangled sob Arabel turned from the bed to the
nearest window. Holding back the curtain, she stood

aside so that her sister could see the sun making a dazzling sweep of light across a sea which lay as smooth as glass.

"Look, Ba, a sea like this could hurt nobody!"

But Ba's heavy eyes were searching the horizon for a sail which would never appear.

She knew the truth then, with a dreadful finality, but for two more terrible days the sisters hoped—prayed— waited. Then they sent for their father. By now they knew the agonizing fact. For some reason the *Belle* had capsized and the three young men had drowned. Edward Barrett's body was the first to float to shore. Captain Clarke was found with the flowers which Arabel had so laughingly given him still fastened in his buttonhole.

There were no tears left for Ba now. She could only cling to her father and look up at him with haunted eyes and say in a ghost of a voice, "Papa—I was selfish—selfish! *I* kept him here to go to his death! Papa, will you—can you forgive?"

Mr. Barrett bent and kissed her, but he said nothing, and Mr. Barrett's silences sometimes were unendurable torture. He was patient and gentle in tending his daughter, but he made no attempt to conceal his grief, or the fact that he held Ba directly responsible for the tragedy.

For months Ba was too weak and too crushed to pray. It was the only time in her life when utter, absolute despair possessed her. And always, night and day, there was the sound of the sea. Whether it murmured mournfully or rose with a savage roar, the sound was always the same in Ba's ears. "Bro is gone! Gone! Gone!"

She came upon a few lines of Robert Browning's and,

years afterwards, told him that nothing he had ever written had lived with her like the lines:

> What says the body when they spring
> Some monstrous torture-engine's whole
> Strength on it? No more says the soul

It was fifteen months before she had strength enough to be taken back to Wimpole Street, and when she did reach her own room, she admitted the chances were she would never leave it again. Gradually she was fighting her way out of the utter desolation she had been plunged into by the Torquay tragedy. She wrote poetry again, she taught herself to smile, to seem to be gay, to take a quick interest in everything she heard or read about, but she knew that everybody agreed that Elizabeth Barrett could never be anything except a hopeless invalid.

Her father never accused or reproached her. In fact he was very kind to her in his own fashion, but she knew, in dozens of ways, that he considered her illness a direct punishment for her sin of willful selfishness.

She was surrounded by love and luxuries and tender care, but John Kenyon certainly was right when, four years later, he came to the conclusion that there was no hope in her room.

*A*T the first sound of footsteps on the stairs Elizabeth's head lifted in a half-apprehensive, questioning movement. Was it Papa, so early? Then unconsciously she relaxed. No, those running feet were not dear Papa's. They must belong to her brother Octavius, whose room was two flights above hers in the high, old Barrett house. He might not even look in on her now, but wait until he was ready to go to dinner. No, the steps were turning down the hallway toward her door.

His knock was quick and staccato.

Elizabeth raised her husky voice. "Come in, Occy, please. Wilson is downstairs."

The door opened and her brother stood still until he was accustomed to the dimness of the room.

" 'Pon my soul, Ba, it smacks of sorcery the way you salute a person by name when he's on the other side of the door. Is it second sight? Will we be having you prophesying shipwrecks next like Miss Martineau's maid?"

He laughed delightedly at his sister's horrified face, and after a moment Elizabeth laughed a little herself. She shook her dark curls. "No, no witchcraft for me, thank you. But when one lives so much of one's life shut-up and alone, each little sound comes to mean something special. I always know who is coming up the stairs, and even the way you knock is different from Arabel or Stormie or Sette. Sometimes I even know whether the day has gone well with you or not, by your way of knocking."

Occy pretended to draw back. "And that isn't sorcery?" His eyes laughed at her. "Well, then, tell me, have things gone well or ill with me today?" he was challenging her when the sound of rustling skirts and light feet caused him to hold up a finger. "Who may that be, O wise Ba?"

"Henrietta!" His sister's eyes twinkled. "And Wilson, of course."

The flourish with which Occy swung the door wide to admit his sister Henrietta and behind her Elizabeth's personal maid, Wilson, bearing a covered tray, would have been a credit to Windsor Castle itself.

"Entrez, mesdemoiselles! Your coming was foretold!"

Ordinarily Henrietta was the quickest to respond to her brother's banter, but tonight it was evident she had not even heard it. She was dressed for dinner, and the high color in her cheeks matched the crimson of her gown. Her breathing was rapid and uneven and she looked half-fearful and half-rebellious.

"I won't be coming to you after dinner tonight, Ba. I'm sorry dear, but Papa has a guest for dinner, and he has just this minute informed me I am to play and sing for him afterward. It's a pity, but there's no escape. I promise to look in on my way to bed, if you're not asleep. And oh, Ba—" Her voice hurried a little and she glanced cautiously toward the door. "When Papa comes here tonight, do try to say or do something to put him in a good humor. You —you can always turn his smooth side out."

Occy surveyed his nervous sister with inquiring sympathy and the little figure on the sofa stiffened in alarm.

"Henrietta, have you done something to displease Papa —again?"

"I—well—he saw Surtees Cook in the music room this afternoon."

"Oh, Henrietta!" Ba cried reproachfully, "how could you be so rash—and right after last week's trouble, too?"

Henrietta gulped. "Papa came home so early. But I thought—I thought he might be pleased, because if he saw Captain Cook, he might take it as a sign I d-didn't c-care about Mr. P-Palfrey—"

Occy made an odd sound, between a snort and a short laugh, and Ba's fingers went to her throat. Nervousness did usually rob her of her voice, even now, and she barely managed to whisper, "Henrietta, do try to placate—" when an imperious summons sent Wilson scurrying to the door.

Edward Barrett strode just far enough inside the room to permit Wilson to close the door softly and swiftly. He was not an especially tall man, but his domineering personality made him seem formidable. His facial expression could be mild enough, but there was a piercing iciness in his eyes which could turn every one of his children, even the adored Elizabeth, cold and breathless.

Tonight he let his glance go from Wilson to Henrietta and on to Occy, who still stood in the middle of the room, and so back to Wilson. And all three were suddenly aware of a disquieting sense of guilt for which none of them could account until he enlightened them.

"Just now I discovered the door of this room ajar—by at least two inches. And I have strictly commanded every member of my household to close it securely. Wilson, is this a piece of your negligence?"

"It is not, sir," Occy said firmly before Wilson could muster words. "I was here with Ba, and I opened the door for my sister and Wilson. Wilson was carrying Ba's tray, so I made haste to close the door, tightly, as I thought—"

His father caught him up grimly. "'As you thought'! You are fully aware of the frail state of your sister's health. I have told you all that Dr. Chambers warned me a chill breath of air would be tragic. Your carelessness might have—"

"Oh, dear Papa, please, please!" Elizabeth was begging breathlessly, "He did no harm. I haven't felt a breath of air."

"I do hope you haven't, love." Her father's voice was all

gentleness as he turned toward her. Wheeling around to his son, he ordered sharply, "Occy, get up to your own room and prepare for dinner. And hasten. We have a guest and I will not wait for you. So unless you enjoy cold roast—Henrietta, I do not choose to bring any unpleasantness into this room, nor will I mention disagreeable matters before dinner. What I have to say to you will keep until morning."

He swung around to seek out Wilson, busy with some unobtrusive occupation in a far corner. "Wilson!"

"Y-yes, sir?"

"You remember the orders Mrs. Robinson gave you from me?"

"Yes, sir. Thank you, sir." The girl bobbed.

"Good. See to it that you follow them." He moved to the sofa and was smiling when he stooped to kiss Elizabeth gently. Then he pinched her cheek. "You look bewildered, Puss, and I don't wonder. But I have seen two or three of your trays as they came downstairs these last few days, and Wilson admits you are not eating well." He shook a playful finger at her. "It must be remedied at once. So Wilson has orders to see that you dispose of every mouthful. I expect a good report from her, my dear."

But Elizabeth had been struggling with a teasing headache and an irritated chest all day. It would almost be torture to eat. She realized from experience that protests were not likely to influence Mr. Barrett, but she heard herself exclaiming, "Oh, Papa dear—it is the east wind and the rain we've been having. My cough is always much

worse in an east wind, and no one could cough and eat
at the same time."

Nothing could have been more gentle than Mr. Barrett's hand as he smoothed her hair. "Nonsense, Ba! You
must eat to gain strength to subdue the cough. Mind
now."

When the door had closed on the last of them, Elizabeth let herself sink into the pillows and her eyes fluttered shut. It had been a dispiriting day. Rain and wind
had beaten against her windows, and set the ivy fretting
against the panes. Usually she was grateful to her cousin
John Kenyon for his gift of the ivy which climbed from
her window ledge to Henrietta's on the next story. Even
in winter it was a proof of green and living things, defy-
ing the dinginess of the London roofs and the sullenness
of the London winter sky, but today the sound of the
brittle leaves beating fitfully against the wet panes had
been mournful beyond belief.

It surprised and disturbed her when she remembered
how sharply everything had seemed to prick at her nerves
today—the dreary, unceasing plashing of the rain, the
shivering sound of the wind, the rasping creak of her
closet door, the lumpish pudding at noontime—on and
on.

Ba was so used to pain and weakness and the cough
which had shaken her today was such a long-time acquaintance that she had come to think of both of them
as quite as much a part of herself as her dark hair. She had
even come to take for granted that lying in this one room
was to be her life. She had accepted that long ago. But as

long as she could read, write letters, and work out her
poetry, she had thought she lived in a very satisfying
world.

But why had everything today set her teeth on edge?
She was ashamed at her nervousness and restlessness. She
had a sudden memory of the sleepy little animals she and
her brother Edward used to uncover in the gardens at
Hope End. She should really have been a dormouse, able
to curl up and hide from the world.

"Your dinner is served, miss," Wilson's respectful voice
was saying. "Shall I prop you up a bit now?"

At the same time something wet and rough touched
Ba's chin. Her eyes came open and she smiled fleetingly,
reflecting that, had she been a dormouse, Flush's attentions wouldn't have been so enjoyable. She cupped the
little head of the toy King Charles spaniel in her hands,
and the large eyes looked back at her wisely.

"Is Flush ready to have his dinner served too?" When
the small creature wagged his tail in a vehement affirma-
tive, she laughed aloud. "What have we to tempt Flush
tonight, Wilson?"

"A wee bit of the meat, and a spot of the cottage cheese,
miss?" Wilson suggested soberly, though her eyes glinted
with amusement, and Ba's had an answering spark. "The
cheese, by all means. Watch here, Flush. See what Miss
Barrett gives you in your dish." Bending over, she placed a
lavish spoonful in the purple bowl beside the sofa. "There.
There's something in Flushie's own bowl that good Mr.
Kenyon gave him."

Flush approached the bowl daintily, took one disdainful

sniff at the proffered cheese and then raised reproachful
eyes to his mistress.

"Good cheese, Flush! Come, come, eat Miss Barrett's
nice cheese," urged Ba gravely.

Flush apparently had other ideas. He produced a minia-
ture growl, shook his silky ears, and continued to stare
pathetically at Elizabeth.

"Might it be the salt he craves, miss?" Wilson suggested
innocently.

"Oh, salt! Did you want your cheese salted, Flush?"
Elizabeth lifted the salt dish from her tray and sprinkled
the contents of the purple bowl vigorously. Whereupon,
having watched her intently, the little spaniel fell upon
the bowl greedily.

"Isn't he clever?" Elizabeth demanded, as though Flush
had developed a new trick instead of exhibiting an old
one. Wilson agreed, "He's a canny one!" And then murmured under her breath, "Canny enough to stay hidden in
the shawls at Miss Ba's feet the whole time the master was
here."

The cheese was followed by a portion of the mutton
from Elizabeth's plate, and finished off with coffee and
sugared cream. Elizabeth's own dinner went in a much
slower fashion. The broth was steaming and savory, and
she tried to eat the rest dutifully, but most of the meal
seemed heavy and unappetizing. Poor Wilson was torn
between her sympathy for Elizabeth and the awful prospect of standing before Mr. Barrett and reporting on the
success of Elizabeth's dinner.

"Oh, miss, you don't take as much as Flush!" she broke

out despairingly. Her mistress bravely tried a few more forkfuls, and then had a fit of coughing and shook her head.

For a second Wilson stood irresolute, then she seized the plate from the tray and placed it on the floor with a determined hand.

"Master's order was that I was to see you dispose of every mouthful, miss. Not a word was said about eating it!"

"Oh, Wilson do you think—isn't it deceiving Papa?"

Wilson's Scotch face was firm. "You'll be disposing of it, miss. Come, Flushie. Good dog!"

Fifteen minutes later Elizabeth watched her bear the empty tray away. Somehow the very stiffness of the maid's back seemed admirable to Miss Barrett.

Wilson was carrying a small silver salver piled with several envelopes when she returned. "The evening post had just come in, Miss Ba."

Elizabeth stretched her hands out eagerly. She was never too tired to receive letters. Sometimes she felt she lived in a world made up of the letters she received and wrote. When she wrote letters she could be the kind of person she would have liked to be if she hadn't had such a bottled-up type of life.

Letting the letters slip through her fingers, she spied one from Miss Mitford. That would be chatty and spicy. Mr. Horne's would probably contain some of his new poems. Mrs. Martin—she was an old friend of the Barrett family. One envelope bore unfamiliar spidery handwriting and the address "Miss Barrett, 50 Wimpole St., London." Elizabeth observed the postmark. "New Cross, Hatcham, January 10, 1845." No one she knew. Perhaps someone who wanted an autograph.

She opened Miss Mitford's letter first. As usual, the finely written sheets were crammed with gossip and quaint observations. Elizabeth smiled as she rearranged the sheets in their proper order. It was almost like having Miss Mitford sit beside her.

Then she chose the letter from Hatcham. She opened it idly enough, but before she had read to the end of the first sentence she was sitting straighter, her breath coming faster. This was not what Miss Barrett would have called an ordinary letter:

I love your verses with all my heart, dear Miss Barrett, —and this is no off-hand complimentary letter that I shall write,—whatever else, no prompt matter-of-course recognition of your genius, and there a graceful and natural end of the thing. Since the day last week when I first read your poems, I quite laugh to remember how I have been turning and turning again in my mind what I should be able to tell you of their effect upon me, for in the first flush of delight, I thought I would this once get out of my habit of purely passive enjoyment, when I do really enjoy, and thoroughly justify my admiration—perhaps even, as a loyal fellow-craftsman should, try and find fault and do you some little good to be proud of hereafter!—but nothing comes of it all—so into me has it gone, and part of me has it become, this great living poetry of yours, not a flower of which but took root and grew—Oh, how different that is from lying to be dried and pressed flat, and prized highly, and put in a book . . . the fresh strange music, the affluent language, the exquisite pathos and true new brave thought; but in this addressing myself to you —your own self, and for the first time, my feeling rises altogether. I do, as I say, love these books with all my heart—and I love you too. Do you know I was once not very far from seeing—really seeing you? Mr. Kenyon said to me one morning "Would you like to see Miss Barrett?" then he went to announce me,—then he returned . . . you were too unwell, and now it is years ago, and I feel as at some untoward passage in my travels, as if I had been close, so close, to some world's-wonder in chapel or crypt, only a screen to push and I might have entered . . . the half-opened door shut and I went home . . . and the sight was never to be?

Well, these Poems were to be, and this true thankful joy and pride with which I feel myself

Yours ever faithfully, Robert Browning

No, this certainly did not resemble any other letter Elizabeth Barrett had ever received. In spite of her walled-in life she could claim several masculine correspondents— Mr. Kenyon of course, blind Mr. Boyd, the artist Benjamin Haydon and the man with whom she had collaborated, Richard Horne. But none of them had ever written her a letter which made her head whirl like this.

By the time she had steadied herself to read it for the third time, certain sentences seemed to spring up from the paper:

This is no off-hand complimentary letter that I shall write—

(It was not, indeed!)

So into me has it gone, and part of me has it become,
this great living poetry of yours—
The fresh strange music, the true, new brave thought—
I love these books with all my heart—and I love you
too—

Still clutching the single sheet, Elizabeth lay back and
raised her eyes to her "Poets' Corner" where she had hung
five engravings of England's most modern poets. The
clean-cut face of Robert Browning looked back at her. She
knew that some people considered his poetry muddled
and uncouth. But she believed he was a genius and the
greatest poet England had possessed since Shakespeare.
Once, when Mr. Kenyon told her Robert Browning had
praised a magazine article she had written, she was
thrilled enough to repeat it in her letters.

Yes, she remembered now that John Kenyon had urged
her to let him bring Mr. Browning to call, but her stubborn shyness always made her refuse. Looking up at the
picture of Browning, Elizabeth was convinced she had
been right not to allow him to come, just as she had always
evaded seeing Richard Horne or Benjamin Haydon. It
really was so much easier on everyone to let them know
only the Elizabeth Barrett who could write a whimsical,
vivid letter with much less effort than she could say ten
words to a visitor. She knew from Mr. Kenyon that Robert
Browning was vigorous, popular wherever he went, and
had traveled in Italy. If he had come and found a small
person wrapped in shawls on her sofa, a person who was
nothing to look at and who would probably have been

tongue-tied with nervousness, he would surely have felt he had wandered into—what was it he said? "A crypt."

How could anyone who had never seen this room have used exactly the right word for it? It was a crypt! Elizabeth looked around it with a sudden shuddering distaste, feeling as if she were seeing it as a stranger would for the first time. The walls had been papered a reddish dark brown, not a cheerful color, but, as Papa had remarked, "a durable one for an invalid's room." The washstand masqueraded as a cabinet. The sofa in reality was a disguised bed; the naturally dull room was made several degrees more dreary by heavy green damask curtains at the windows. And of course the windows were never opened. In fact, because it was winter, at present they were sealed shut with brown paper. Once she had fainted when she was being lifted from her sofa to a chair, and Papa had promptly attributed the disaster to an open window, whereupon the decree went forth against opened windows.

In a bowl on her little table the potted primroses which John Kenyon had brought her two days before drooped pathetically.

Poor flowers! thought Elizabeth ruefully, even you can't breathe in the atmosphere ordained for me.

One could fairly taste the bleakness in this room. Oh, she had been perfectly right not to let Mr. Browning come. She would write him, of course she would write him. But he must never, never visit her in this—this crypt.

After Wilson had settled her for the night, she lay listening for Henrietta's footsteps, but they did not come. Prob-

ably it was just as well. Naturally she would tell both
Henrietta and Arabel about Mr. Browning's letter. Henrietta, especially, would be interested. She had seen him
dancing at a ball not long ago and had given her sisters a
glowing account of how gracefully he "polked." But to
Elizabeth Barrett he wasn't the charming, exciting man-
about-town; he was a person whose ability she considered
boundless and whose opinion she trusted, whose admiration rang true in her ears, and whose letter had been like
the clasp of an understanding hand.

I love these books with all my heart, the phrase sang
over and over in her mind, and then, almost in her sleep
she heard the end of the sentence:

—and I love you too!

*W*AKING to as much sunlight as was permitted to filter through the thick green damask draperies, Elizabeth had an odd sensation, as though something warm and fresh and radiant had passed over her and still lingered in the air. As a child she had frequently waked with this buoyant feeling of delight and exultation, and she remembered how she would leap from bed for an early morning ride on her pony Moses or dart to her writing desk to scribble down a poem.

She smiled at the remembrance of the impetuous little Ba Barrett who had galloped over the moor on her pony, the fresh wind lifting her dark curls. It was strange that this curious sensation should visit her now. She thought it had faded with her childhood. Certainly there was nothing in her present life to cause this stirring of exultation.

Her eye caught the letter on her bedside table, where she had left it last night. Ah, yes, Mr. Browning's letter. She sat more erect and reached for it, curious to see if it would still move her as it had last night. Things seen by candlelight sometimes did not look the same by day.

She was reading the letter for the second time when Wilson entered with the articles for her bath. Thoughtfully Ba placed the envelope in the private drawer of the table. It was just as straightforward and sincere as it had been last night. She must answer Mr. Browning immediately after breakfast.

Ba planned her letter over her breakfast tray, and because she was concentrating on something besides the uninspiring porridge, she surprised and delighted Wilson with the amount she managed to consume.

"You had a rare good appetite this morning, miss!" Wilson beamed on the almost empty bowl.

"It's the sunshine," said her mistress absently. "Please hand me my desk, Wilson."

The reply she wrote on her small, gilt-edged, cream-colored stationery was twice as long as Mr. Browning's letter. She thanked him for his praise and told him how proud she would be for his criticism, not that she pretended to extraordinary meekness under criticism, and she wouldn't promise to obey his. She wrote on and on, and suddenly stopped aghast at what she had said:

Is it indeed true that I was so near to the pleasure and honour of making your acquaintance? and can it be true that you look back upon the lost opportunity with any regret? But—you know—if you had entered the "crypt," you might have caught cold, or been tired to death, and wished *yourself "a thousand miles off"; which would have been worse than travelling them. It is not my interest, however, to put such thoughts in your head about its being "all for the best"; and I would rather hope (as I do) that what I lost by one chance I may recover by some future one. Winters shut me up as they do dormouse's eyes; in the spring* we shall see . . .

She had never intended to write that! It almost amounted to an invitation, and she surely had not changed her resolution not to let Mr. Browning call. Should she tear the sheet up and begin again? Her pen wavered—no, let it stand. Probably Mr. Browning wouldn't give it a second thought, or, if he did press for an invitation, she could find excuses for keeping him away. She dipped her pen again and scribbled hurriedly to the end of the letter.

Arabel, looking demure and beguiling in a dark blue bonnet, came in a couple of hours later to ask if Ba needed any purchases made in the shops.

"Nothing in the shops, thank you, Arabel. But if you wait until I finish this letter to Mrs. Martin, you could drop my letters in the corner box. And oh, I do want you to see this letter which came last night. I liked it so much. It's from Mr. Browning. Cousin John talks of him, you know—" for some reason she was ending on a rather breathless note.

Arabel took the proffered letter and sat down. Elizabeth bent over her writing desk again, but she could detect Arabel's little frown of concentration. At best the Brown-

ing handwriting was peculiar and difficult, and upon first
acquaintance it appeared a jumble of assorted angles.
Arabel lacked her sister's ability to decipher everyone's
handwriting at sight, but when she did glance up her face
held a curious expression.

"Did you really like it, Ba? It sounds so strange! It
doesn't sound like a letter, do you think? It's more—"

"Like speaking. As though he were here speaking to
one," Elizabeth murmured softly, and Arabel nodded in
quick agreement.

"Yes, that's what I mean. Rambling and not properly set
down, you know."

Rambling? Elizabeth nearly leaped from the sofa to
snatch the letter from the misguided Arabel. *Not properly
set down?* Elizabeth's unsteady fingers spilled the hot wax
so that it left an unsightly trail across the envelope addressed to Mrs. Martin. Well, Arabel had Henrietta and
the six brothers to talk with; she had never felt the yearning to know even one person who would see and understand the things Elizabeth did not dare show her everyday family and friends.

"Are you going to see him, Ba?" Arabel really had no
need to ask if she were going to receive Mr. Browning.
Elizabeth gave her the handful of letters and said with
careful emphasis, "No, dear, of course I'm not seeing Mr.
Browning. Why should I?"

Arabel's observant eyes noted the name and address on
the top envelope. She looked amused as she read aloud,
" 'Robert Browning, Esq., New Cross, Hatcham, Surrey.'
You're not a believer in delay, are you, Ba?"

"It's pure courtesy to be prompt to answer a stranger's letter," Elizabeth defended herself.

Arabel Barrett had the low, humble voice which her father said was such an excellent thing in a woman. Her azure eyes were innocent and wide, but Ba sometimes had occasion to wonder if she actually was as guileless as she seemed.

"Mr. Kenyon says that Mr. Browning is noted for achieving whatever he desires," said Arabel's soft little voice as she gathered up her sister's letters and took her departure. For no good reason Elizabeth felt herself blushing.

But the sun had moved from the range of her windows; the delicious warmth which had flooded her at waking had vanished. The familiar feeling of emptiness possessed her once more.

Well, that was all right. Hadn't she said herself that she felt certain advantages in being insulated in her room, and not minding anybody while she wrote her poems? And caring less for criticism or sympathy than she did about the black fly buzzing on the pane?

With the curious instinct by which he always divined when his mistress was in need of diversion or comfort, Flush left the sunny corner where he had been amusing himself to come padding across the room. He paused for the barest second and then leaped to the sofa, his tail a plume of light. The next minute he was licking her hands and lifting his dark eyes questioningly.

Elizabeth caught him up with an almost fierce gesture.

"Oh, Flush, you're worth more to me than all the criticism and praise in the world!" she whispered in his ear.

Apparently Flush agreed with her. He blinked his complacent acknowledgment, once or twice, and then snuggled down in the shawls at her feet.

Mr. Browning's letter lay where Arabel had carelessly dropped it on the little railed table by Elizabeth's side. After her sister's remarks, it struck Elizabeth that it might be just as prudent to keep the letter from unappreciative eyes. She replaced it gently in the envelope and shut it away in the drawer reserved for letters from strangers. Resolutely she shut it out of her mind as well. Just because Mr. Browning had had one brief impulse to write her a generous letter was no cause for her to go into a rapture. She was ashamed to remember how she had ended her letter to Mrs. Martin: "I had a letter from Browning the poet last night, which threw me into ecstasies." And probably Mr. Browning had forgotten the very existence of an invalid like Miss Barrett even before his letter had been delivered at 50 Wimpole Street.

All of which proved she had been quite right when she told her brother Occy that she didn't indulge in sorcery. Certainly she was no prophetess. For in the weeks that followed, Mr. Browning showed no signs of forgetting Miss Barrett's existence, and furthermore he had no intention of letting her forget his.

Arabel had posted Elizabeth's letter on Saturday. By Tuesday night a second missive from Hatcham had arrived, considerably longer than the first. R. Browning had noticed her indiscreet sentence "in the spring we shall see," and ended his second letter gleefully, *I will joyfully wait for the delight of your friendship, and the spring . . .*

But this was only mid-January, spring was months in the future, and meanwhile it might be fascinating to be friends with Robert Browning by letter. He was an expert in her beloved Greek, he knew all the poets and other people she had only heard or read about, he had traveled on the Continent, and had a trick of writing about them as though Elizabeth were sharing his experiences. And nothing in the world came more naturally to Elizabeth herself than writing letters. Why shouldn't she enjoy Mr. Browning's friendship in this way?

Before six weeks had passed she couldn't disguise the fact that she was enjoying it. She caught herself watching for the post, and was surprised at the stab of disappointment if a letter from New Cross, Hatcham didn't arrive when she expected it. When Wilson brought up her letters she formed the habit of riffling through them rapidly for a glimpse of the spidery Browning handwriting.

Wilson's controlled face never made her nervous, but it grew to be a different story if one of her sisters carried the mail to her or was present when she received it. Henrietta took to keeping Mr. Browning's envelope until last and then, when Elizabeth was aquiver with suspense, producing it with a flourish and proclaiming, "And one from Hatcham!"

It was also Henrietta who, coming in for her daily visit, would regard her sister intently, and then remark knowingly, "I'm no seeress, but there was a letter from the gentleman of Hatcham today, wasn't there?"

And at Elizabeth's attempted look of wide-eyed inno-

cence, Henrietta would dimple beguilingly, well pleased
with her own discernment. "No, love, you were never
meant for subterfuge. Your face is like crystal! And when
you've had a letter from Mr. Browning, there's a certain
look—"

To say "Now, Henrietta, please don't imagine causes!"
was a feeble retreat.

With Arabel it was worse. Elizabeth would try to appear unconcerned at the sight of the now familiar envelope, but the merriment in Arabel's blue eyes usually
betrayed her into blushing, especially when her sister
inquired solicitously, "Is poor Mr. Browning quite convinced by now that you are never going to grant him the
favor of a call?"

As for Mr. Browning himself, in the midst of writing
about Italy or the ancient Greeks, or exchanging criticisms
and notes on each other's poetry, in almost every letter he
scattered a few words about the oncoming Spring—with
a capital *S*.

On the 26th of February he dated his letter:

Wednesday morning—Spring!
Real warm Spring, dear Miss Barrett, and the birds know
it; and in Spring I shall see you, surely see you—for
when did I once fail to get whatever I had set my heart
upon?

Papa certainly would frown upon this boasting senti-
ment, Elizabeth realized instinctively, only coming from
Mr. Browning, somehow, it didn't seem like boasting.
This would have been the exact moment for her to have
written a tactful, but firm, note, giving Mr. Browning to

understand once and for all that, while she would be delighted to be his friend-by-letter for years, they were never to meet.

But the letter she sent back did not read that way:

Yes, but, dear Mr. Browning, I want the spring according to the new "style" (mine), and not the old one of you and the rest of the poets. To me unhappily, the snowdrop is much the same as the snow—it feels as cold underfoot— and I have grown sceptical about "the voice of the turtle," the east winds blow so loud. April is a Parthian with a dart, and May (at least the early part of it) a spy in the camp. That is my idea of what you call spring.

Perhaps, Elizabeth reflected, it would be better and kinder to discourage Mr. Browning by gentle means, rather than by a blunt message. But the exuberant Robert didn't admit discouragement when he met it. He continued to write gaily of spring:

Surely the wind that sets my chestnut-tree dancing, all its baby-cone-blossoms, green now, rocking like fairy castles on a hill in an earthquake,—that is South West, surely!

Elizabeth shut her eyes and remembered the chestnut trees in the park at Hope End where she had raced with her brother Edward when she was a girl. Almost she had forgotten there were such things as baby-cone-blossoms.

She had noticed before that she and Mr. Browning were impressed by the same things.

But Mr. Browning wasn't above using subtle and frightening tactics to get what he desired. He took to writing vaguely about going abroad to new countries. The thought gave Miss Barrett a parched sensation, like the taste of bitter medicine.

If you mean "to travel," she wrote back, *why, I shall have to miss you.* And then she added wistfully, *Do you really mean it?*

Now that it was May, the thought of missing the intimate letters that came almost every other day was as chilling as her hated east wind.

It had been very well to talk about the "advantage of being insulated from other people," but suddenly Ba was forced to acknowledge to herself that she didn't want to be insulated against Robert Browning.

Afterward she often wondered just when she began to admit that seeing him was inevitable. She knew she had been holding the idea at bay for several weeks, perhaps even months.

Early in May Mr. Kenyon decided to give a dinner party for his favorite friends. He invited Miss Sarianna Browning and Mr. Robert Browning, together with Miss Henrietta Barrett and Mr. George Barrett. Robert Browning had no desire to meet any of the Barrett family except Elizabeth. He pleaded a bad headache and stayed in Hatcham. The rotund Mr. Kenyon was both disappointed and concerned when he reported his failure to Elizabeth. It was so unlike Robert Browning to be ill. A flash of startled intuition darted across Elizabeth's mind and at eleven o'clock that Sunday night she wrote a troubled, very hurried note.

May I ask how the head is? . . . Mr. Kenyon was here to-day and told me such bad news that I cannot sleep to-

*night . . . without asking such a question as this, dear Mr.
Browning.*

*Let me hear how you are—Will you? and let me hear (if
I can) that it was prudence or some unchristian virtue
. . . which made you put aside the engagement for Tuesday. . . . I had been thinking so of seeing you on Tuesday
. . . with my sister's eyes—for the first sight.*

A few days earlier she had scribbled a hasty sentence
which must have set all the bells in the world ringing for
the impulsive Robert Browning. *Shall I have courage to
see you soon, I wonder! If you ask me, I must ask myself.*

In his study in Hatcham, with the windows open to the
soft May wind and the delicate spring fragrance, Browning wrote that his headache had been due to too many late
hours. And then, after rambling for a page or two about
nothing important, he came abruptly to the point. *When
I am to see you—I will never ask you! . . . I ask you not to
see me so long as you are unwell, or mistrustful. . . .*

Once more panic seized Ba. Here was a man who would
never be content with impersonal letters, much as they
had come to mean to her. She had warded him off because
she honestly believed he would be so desperately disappointed after he had once seen her, that it would mean
the end of their friendship. He would never talk of coming again. She was little and sick, fit only for the dark. She
had never learned to act or talk the way people did in
London. And not the least straw of pleasure could come to
Mr. Browning from meeting her.

But she was too headlong a spirit to ignore the challenge
in Mr. Browning's latest letter. She would tell him hon-

estly why she had put him off, and invite him definitely.
At last it was done.

*I will see you . . . any day after two, or before six. And
my sister will bring you up stairs to me; and we will talk;
or you will talk; and you will try to be indulgent, and like
me as well as you can.*

That night Mr. Barrett observed the warning signs in
his daughter's face, flaming cheeks, red-rimmed eyes, and
cold hands. Kneeling beside her bed he fervently asked
Heaven to grant her a merciful relief from her weariness
and pain.

Mr. Barrett would have been shocked if anyone had
suggested later that his petition had been speedily answered in the form of a letter to Ba.

*Dear Miss Barrett, I thank you for the leave you give me
. . . I will call at 2 on Tuesday. . . .*

                                        Ever yours, R.B.

$\mathcal{E}$LIZABETH watched Wilson give last minute company touches to her bed-sitting-room. If she had been expecting the door to admit Dr. Chambers and one of the solemn-faced specialists who occasionally came to plague her with new examinations, she couldn't have been more shrinking and tense, she reflected.

And then the imp of humor, which always danced in Elizabeth Barrett under the dreariest conditions, lifted its head. For what specialist, even the most noted in England, would Wilson have insisted that her mistress wear her most becoming gown of cinnamon velvet with deep lace at the throat and wrists? Or brushed the long ringlets until each curl had a special sheen, and Elizabeth felt obliged to protest?

"There's no need for all this finery, Wilson! You can't make me beautiful, you know."

"No, miss," Wilson agreed meekly, taking up the tiny vial of perfume from the railed stand and touching the smallest drop to the soft hair. "That's an act of Providence, miss."

Elizabeth started, stared, and then turned the subject.

"Will you look at the clock, please, Wilson, and see how much time we have before—before the hour strikes?"

"Yes, miss! Certainly." For the seventh time since noon Wilson disappeared into the corridor to consult the stairway clock. There had been no watch or clock in Ba's possession since Mr. Barrett had decided, three years before, that the sight and sound of any timepiece was too trying for an invalid's nerves. Usually time didn't matter in the sepia room, but today—Ba was ashamed how frequently she had dispatched poor Wilson to the stair landing.

"It is precisely twenty-four minutes past two, miss."

Miss Barrett's lips moved in a way that was meant to be "Thank you."

Thirty-six more minutes of waiting to be endured. Why hadn't she permitted him to come at two, the hour he had named in his note? Her reason was that one or two of her brothers might still be in the house at two o'clock, and she shrank from the unmerciful teasing which would surely follow if Occy or Sette knew she had received a popular man-about-London like Robert Browning. But this interminable waiting—thirty-six—well, possibly thirty-one more minutes—

Wilson was eying her too sympathetically. Ba straightened.

"I believe you and Miss Henrietta agreed it is a pleasant day?"

"Indeed yes, miss!" Wilson's neat cap bobbed in quick assent. "It's a fine day, sunny and balmy, and the sky soft-like. The gentleman has a rare day for coming up to London." To herself Lily Wilson was adding, "and a rare good omen too."

"Mr.—anyone coming from the fresh countryside would certainly find this room intolerably warm and stuffy," Ba said wistfully. "You can't deny that the air is close in here, Wilson, and Mr. Browning has been suffering from headaches. We must open up one or two windows immediately."

For once the discreet Wilson lost her disciplined expression. Open Miss Ba's windows—in May? If the city lay blanketed in heat during mid-summer, sometimes it was permitted, but never in May, even with the month at its mildest. And a certain dire memory struck Wilson.

"You remember, miss, how you fainted last time we opened a window?"

"That was months ago!" Ba's expressive hands dismissed the episode. "In December, I remember, with a raw, east wind, and you opened the window to be rid of the smoke from the fireplace. If today is as bland as you say, it will do me good to breathe a little air."

"I'd best be brushing and combing Flush now, miss."

"See to the windows first, if you please."

Lily Wilson cast a longing look at the door as though

she were tempted to summon help in dealing with her willful mistress. Under all her soft ways Ba had a firm stratum of the Barrett rocklike obstinacy and determination. Wilson tried to smother her qualms and reluctantly approached the windows, wrestling with them until they grudgingly yielded a few inches.

The flowers on the table nodded a little in the welcome air, and Ba put up her hand to touch her cheek where the breeze had touched it. She had forgotten the May wind could be so soft and fragrant, even in London. She turned to speak comfortingly to Flush, who was growling irritably under Wilson's combing, and her eyes widened in dismay at sight of her "Poets' Corner."

"Good gracious! Wilson, be quick! Take down Mr. Browning's picture! It would never do to let him know he had been hung between Tennyson and Wordsworth." She beat her hands together in a flurry of impatience. "Hurry!" She surveyed Wilson's maneuvers with a strained expression. "Is there too noticeable a space between the portraits now?"

"I can move Mr. Wordsworth and Mr. Tennyson a wee bit nearer to each other," said Wilson soothingly. "Now where shall I hide Mr. Browning?"

The word "hide" caused Ba a guilty qualm. But what else was she doing? "Put him—put him under the copy of 'Sordello.' " Ba finished with a little rush of relief. No poet would ever lift a copy of his own work.

In the corridor was the muted sound of three chiming notes from the clock, and then the sound of steps. Henrietta's light feet and the hurrying feet of someone else.

The eyes of mistress and maid met in quick understanding.

"You won't be needing me now, miss," Wilson said softly.

"No," breathed Ba.

Fully a minute must have gone by after Wilson cautiously slipped out before Henrietta turned the knob of the door. Henrietta stayed only long enough to say in her clear voice, "Mr. Browning, Ba," before she, too, retreated, and Ba was left to face the person whose determination had beaten down her own.

"The calendar claims today is the twentieth of May." Mr. Browning began talking even as he crossed the threshold and strode to the sofa. "But I'm counting this as the first day of spring, dear Miss Barrett!" His voice was deep, like a low-toned bell, and the eyes which met Ba's were sea-blue. His handclasp was firmer than anyone had given Elizabeth Barrett for many years. Indeed, Mr. Browning was filled with more vitality and eagerness than anyone she had ever seen in Wimpole Street.

Not above medium height, her caller had very broad shoulders, a very tanned face which accentuated his clean-cut good looks, dark hair, and extremely well-tailored clothes.

For his part, looking down at his hostess, Robert Browning beheld a slight person with a delicate face framed in very dark shoulder-length curls, a full-lipped, tender mouth, and what he himself later called "spirit hands." But it was Elizabeth Barrett's eyes which claimed his attention, and which he remembered all his life. "Eyes of various colours as the sun shines,—called blue and black, ... affidavit-ed for gray—sworn at for hazel" and set down by Ba herself as "dark-green-brown." Fringed with long lashes, they were wistful and gallant and eager as they looked at Robert Browning for the first time, and the forthright Robert answered their look.

"Now, Miss Barrett, please trust me. I promise I won't walk off with the family umbrellas and coats in the hall, nor will I write an article for *Colborn's Magazine* on any of your sayings or doings." He grinned at her, and Wilson or any of the Barretts would have been startled by an unfamiliar sound. Elizabeth Barrett was laughing.

"Do be seated, please, Mr. Browning." It was fortunate that Mr. Browning had the gift of a ready tongue, for her throat had felt positively locked, and even now her voice sounded uneven and hurried in her own ears.

Mr. Browning turned, surveyed the room, and walked to the low seat placed opposite the sofa as casually as though he had been used to Miss Barrett's bed-sitting-room all his life. "Thank you, I will take the gondola chair." He settled himself and leaned forward with another smile—no, "smile" was too moderate a word for the lighting of Mr. Browning's expressive face. Ba had to admit to herself that he grinned, and somehow it was a very engaging grin.

"It is high time you saw me, for I have clearly written myself out in my letters—"

"Mr. Browning—" (and here was another surprising thing, that Elizabeth should be guilty of interrupting) "I feel ashamed for having made a fuss about something that was not worth it. I cannot admit visitors in a general way, but putting the question of health aside, it would be unbecoming to lie here on the sofa and make a company show of my infirmity."

"Oh!" said Mr. Browning gravely, "am I a 'general' visitor?"

Elizabeth blushed. Perhaps she made a nervous movement which woke her dog. He sat up, scrutinized the unfamiliar occupant of the "gondola chair" disapprovingly, and then gave an unmistakable growl.

"Oh, Flush, be quiet! What a greeting to give Mr. Browning!"

"He'll do better as our acquaintance improves," remarked Mr. Browning calmly. He made no overtures to Flush, and didn't address him in the sticky, cajoling tone which a few of her guests had used to the obviously disgusted spaniel.

"We will see more of each other, you and I? You said in one of your letters, 'come then. There will be truth and simplicity for you in any case, and a friend.' If you meant that, I would be proud and honored. As for your 'infirmity,' it hasn't hindered your writing the strongest, finest, new poetry in England today, so I can't see why you should hold it over my head, and say, 'See, this is why we can't enjoy a face-to-face friendship.' Dear Miss Barrett, I don't give a fig for your infirmity, but I care everything in the world for your friendship and your help. May I have them?"

This certainly wasn't the variety of conversation Ba was used to hearing from her visitors. It wasn't in the least like the usual we-must-be-careful-and-cheerful-about-what-we-say-to-poor-Ba strain of talk she usually heard. Obviously Mr. Browning didn't understand how one should treat an invalid. Ba felt as though someone had opened all her windows to a fresh, clean, strong breeze, and after her first start, she was astonished at the exhilaration which swept over her.

She could even talk to Mr. Browning in a way she never had talked to Mr. Kenyon or Miss Mitford, although afterward she searched her memory in vain to recall what they had talked about.

When the clock chimed four-thirty, and Mr. Browning rose to go, he suddenly looked a little guilty.

"Are you tired? Did I stay too long? Did I do anything wrong? For instance, at home they all say I speak very loud."

The dark ringlets shook in swift reassurance. "Indeed there was nothing wrong. How could there be?" It gave Ba a distinctly odd sensation to have this brilliant poet, playwright, and world traveler searching her face with such humble anxiety. She smiled at him blithely. "And there was everything right, why shouldn't there be? As for the 'loud speaking,' I didn't hear any!"

She was about to ring for Wilson, when she heard herself saying, "You will really come next Tuesday?"

Joy flashed from Robert Browning's blue eyes. He knew he had succeeded in breaking through the shield of fears Elizabeth had used to ward him off, but he had no intention of forfeiting his gains by too impulsive an answer.

"I will come on Tuesday, and again whenever you like."

It was Henrietta who came to usher Mr. Browning downstairs, a Henrietta so plainly consumed with curiosity that she must have practically shut the door on Mr. Browning's back in order to dart back up the two flights of stairs and flounce into her sister's room.

"Oh, Ba! What did you say? What did you do? How long he stayed! Arabel was just about to break in and tell him—delicately, of course—that you weren't allowed visitors for more than half an hour a day, but when she came to the door, she heard you laughing—Oh, Ba, are you so tired, dear, that you don't hear what I'm saying?"

And then she stood stock-still in frightened bewilderment. "Why, Ba!"

Her sister was gazing upon the long, low easy seat Mr. Browning had christened the "gondola chair."

"Seven days," she murmured. "And days are so long this time of year."

*S*O Robert Browning had permission to call upon Ba again. And still again. If something interfered with their Tuesday, Mr. Browning was invited for Wednesday—or Saturday—or Monday. And in between times there was always the post.

It was perfectly apparent that Robert Browning did not find Ba "little and sick, fit only for the dark," and by some miracle Ba discovered that she was never shy or afflicted with what she called "a tripping tongue" when Mr. Browning sat in his gondola chair.

Indeed there must have been times when the quick Browning sense of humor was roused by the complete about-face Miss Elizabeth Barrett was making in her letters. Instead of snatching at all the excuses she could concoct to keep him at bay, she was sounding breathless and apologetic if she had to ask him to change the day for his call.

You will think me the most changeable of all the changeable; but indeed it is not my fault that I cannot, as I wished, receive you on Wednesday ... our friends ... come to this house on Tuesday (to-morrow) to pass two or three days, until they settle in an hotel ... but if they go away in time, and if Saturday should suit you, I will let you know by a word; and you can answer by a yea or nay.

But if Mr. Browning did laugh a little over Miss Barrett's frantic apologies, he was wise enough to be discreetly gentle when he answered, telling her that Saturday, Monday, indeed any day she chose, would be perfect for him.

And Ba was obliged to write to him rather shamefacedly:

What will you think when I write to ask you not to come tomorrow, ... but .. on Friday perhaps? And went on to explain that she had tried to change the day of Miss Mitford's visit, but without success; that her aunt, Mrs. Hedley, had notified the Barretts to expect her on Wednesday noon, and finally there had been a note from Mr. Kenyon saying he would call at four o'clock. *So do observe the constellation of adverse stars ... if any harm should happen to Friday, I will write again; but if ... you are able to come then, you will come ...*

This certainly was a different Miss Barrett who had fought so desperately against seeing her friend-by-correspondence.

Mr. Browning sent back a very short note:

Friday is best day because nearest, but Saturday is next best—it is next near, you know: . . . therefore, Friday is my day.

And then, although it was barely a month since his first call, he ventured to sign himself, *Your own R.B.*

But new complications arose, and that particular Friday was not his day. Ba wrote she was tired, but that he could come on Saturday.

Mr. Browning arrived promptly at three. And Ba made no attempt to repress her sigh of relief as he took his place beside her. She could meet the sea-blue eyes directly now, and her fingers no longer trembled in his clasp.

"I snatched at your permission to come, you see, even though my conscience tells me you must be far too tired for another visitor this week. But I won't stay so long nor talk so loud, and if you should feel the least bit tired—"

Ba was shaking her head.

"No, no. I was tired on Wednesday by the confusion of so many voices in this room, but the effect went off, and Miss Mitford was with me for hours yesterday, and I was not worse. No, you can never do me any harm by coming, only give me pleasure. Tell me about the new poems. Did you bring 'The Flight of the Duchess'? I have mine ready for you to take today, and when you come next Tuesday you can use your tomahawk on them, only I don't promise to be meek!"

It was delightful, Henrietta and Arabel told each other, that Ba had finally met someone whose chief interest would always be like her own—poetry. Mr. Kenyon's visits were wonderful and entertaining, but he was always speaking of travel and celebrated people—and sometimes, her sisters suspected, Ba must feel more like a prisoner than ever after his departure. Ba loved little Miss Mitford, but that lady's incessant stream of conversation was likely to be confusing, and more than once an afternoon session with Miss Mitford's tongue had left her tired and sleepless. Her other close friend, Anna Jameson, the Irish author, was a sparkling companion but a bit forthright and tactless for an invalid.

"I tell you, your case is not desperate!" Henrietta had heard her exclaiming emphatically to Ba one day. "When I hear people say 'Circumstances are against me,' I always retort, 'You mean your will is not with you!' Your case isn't desperate, Ba. No woman's is if she wills strongly enough."

But with Mr. Browning Ba was surely safe enough. Even though he was very gay socially, and traveled to France and Italy even more casually than the Barretts would have undertaken a journey to the country, his one thought when he was with Ba naturally would be their poetry.

"Such a nice arrangement," Arabel observed happily to Henrietta one afternoon after she had escorted Mr. Browning to the sepia room. "It's delightful for Ba to know a man like Mr. Browning, and we can depend upon him to talk only poetry, and not to distress Ba or upset her routine."

And marvel of marvels, even Papa approved of his daughter's surprising friendship. And why not? The handsome, vigorous, popular Robert Browning never would be interested in Ba as a person. Mr. Barrett thought it perfectly right and proper that Robert Browning, the poet, should come to acknowledge and admire Miss Elizabeth Barrett's genius.

It may have been just as well at this stage that no one did know what the two poets talked about. Of course, they did discuss and criticize and praise each other's poetry, but surprisingly soon after that memorable twentieth of May they found an even more interesting topic—themselves.

It was astonishing how very much alike they were. Even to the strange fact that both their families had come from Jamaica. Mr. Barrett had been born there and his wealth came from his Jamaican sugar plantations. Ba never even hinted it, but perhaps she surmised that her father's weird notion of considering his children as possessions was the result of having been surrounded by slaves in his early childhood.

The Brownings had also owned Jamaican sugar plantations managed by slaves, only their story had a different twist. Mr. Barrett had deliberately waited until England passed the law freeing the Negroes of Jamaica, but Robert's father had become disgusted at the thought of being a slaveowner and had freed his slaves of his own accord, dividing his plantation property among them so that they might have a means of earning their living. In consequence, Robert Browning, Sr., had no wealth and worked in the Bank of England, but Ba envied Mr.

Browning for having a father who refused to use people as chattels.

As for Miss Barrett and Mr. Browning themselves, both of them had been petted and encouraged as children; both of them had been making poems long before they could write them down themselves; they both thought of Italy as paradise—Robert Browning because he had lived there and given his heart to the lovely sunny land, and Ba because Italy had been held out before her as a place of health and hope.

Sometimes she was startled when she heard herself telling Browning incidents her own family had never known. Even the understanding Henrietta and Arabel would be shocked if they heard that when she was a child Ba had prayed to the goddess Minerva, and even crept into the garden at Hope End, just as dawn was breaking, with matches stolen from the kitchen to light a sacrifice to Minerva.

Mr. Browning chuckled. "Were you caught? I made a fiery sacrifice myself in my early days, although it was before I heard of the Greek gods. When I was three I burned my mother's Brussels lace veil 'to make a pretty blaze.' I was a fierce male child! I once terrified my poor maiden aunt by greeting her dressed as the devil, wagging a paper tail, when she came to our home on a visit."

Miss Barrett found this story delightful. She lay back and laughed until the tears rolled down her cheeks. Then, seeing Wilson peering around the crack of the door, she hastily gathered her dignity together and put on a sober face. "No, no, Wilson; we are not ready for our tea. You did not hear me ring. Come, Mr. Browning, you haven't told me about your new long poem. 'Luria,' I think it is?"

Well, it seemed "Luria" was being rather stubborn, and giving his author quite a run of trouble. At all events, Mr. Browning was feeling rather bored with him. He preferred talking about Miss Barrett.

"If you made sacrifices to Minerva, you really must have heard about the Greeks early. I was five when I asked my father what he was reading one day, and he said the 'Siege of Troy.' Of course I had to know what a 'siege' and a 'Troy' were, and he took his big books from the shelves to build the walls of Troy and used our family cat to be Helen. I've loved the Greek poets ever since."

"Dear Papa played with me too," Ba said hurriedly. "When I was a small child he would lift me up upon the chimney piece and tell me to stand straight 'like a hero.' And I did, straighter and straighter till suddenly the walls grew alive behind me, and I could feel two stony hands trying to push me down that frightful precipice to the rug where old Havannah, the dog, lay and it seemed we were likely to mix our bones together."

Mr. Browning had heard accounts of Papa before. He made no comment on Miss Barrett's story, but it confirmed the opinion he already had, that he and dear Papa would never see eye to eye. He tactfully changed the subject, managing to hit upon the one thing, had he only known it, which all of Ba's friends and relatives always scrupulously avoided—the matter of getting well.

"I hope that you will have had your great adventure of going downstairs before I come again," he told her. "This perfect June weather was made for that very purpose. And you confess Dr. Chambers has been urging you to try going out for short drives? Well, then—"

"Oh, I am always better in the summer," Ba said lightly. "I emerge from my hibernation and move about a little. But even in summer we have an east wind—" She shrugged and threw out her hands with a smile. "That's just my fate. Now let's talk about something more interesting."

Mr. Browning did not change the subject. "You shall learn to laugh at east winds as I do," he told Ba positively, leaning forward so that his steady eyes held her startled ones. "You are better, you look so and speak so. Only you must seize every opportunity to gather your strength by the handfuls."

"So that I'll have that much more to lose when the first frost strikes me?" Ba countered wryly. "Really, I do well enough just as I am. Why should it be so important for me to be any stronger?"

A sudden flicker in the intense face of her visitor made her flush and feel oddly disturbed. "Don't you really know?" queried Robert Browning gravely.

For some reason his question seemed to echo in the room long after Mr. Browning had departed. She heard it above Flush's excited barks of joy as he returned from his afternoon walk with Wilson, and she seemed to hear it again when a gay and excited Henrietta burst in just before dinner to tell of the marvelous afternoon she had spent with Captain Surtees Cook, and how stunning he looked in his new uniform. Mr. Browning's voice was in

her ears even while Papa knelt at her side and offered his
doleful nightly prayer.

All through the next morning Mr. Browning's short
question disturbed Ba at intervals. From the time of Bro's
death no one had so much as suggested she might or could
get well. None of the Barretts would have ventured to
question Papa's conviction that Ba's illness was an act of
God, from which there could be no escape. John Kenyon,
sympathetic and understanding though he was, usually
was inclined to take things just as they were; Mary Russell
Mitford had long ago accepted her friend's invalidism as
a perfectly natural thing. Only the blunt, outspoken Mrs.
Jameson had even suggested the possibility of Ba's getting
better, and with the odds so overwhelmingly against it, Ba
had dismissed Mrs. Jameson's views as a hopeful theory.

But Mr. Browning's talk was an altogether different
matter. After hearing nightly prayers about a "fading life"
and pleas for the blessing of a speedy release to Heaven,
Ba found it startling to be urged to go out into the June air
and try a tonic of sunshine and flowers!

Resolutely she called Wilson to bring her writing desk.
She would finish the poems the editor of *Blackwood's
Magazine* had requested. She had learned to contrive
poems under any condition. At least she thought she had,
but today—

Today the space of sky which Ba could see was softly,
deeply blue; the breeze which passed through the few
inches of the open window was tantalizingly fragrant; the
yellow roses from Mr. Browning's mother's garden looked
almost as fresh as they had yesterday. Altogether they

wove a kind of challenge, a challenge Ba thought she had forgotten years before.

After half an hour she looked down at the utterly stupid beginnings she had made of three poems, laid down her pen, and then called, "Wilson! Will you tell me the time?"

"A quarter after three, miss," the maid reported after a quick trip to the hallway.

"And would you say the day is really pleasant?"

"Oh, yes, indeed, miss, it is a bonny day!" The ribbons on Wilson's cap danced as she bobbed her head with emphasis.

"Would—would any of my brothers be at home?"

"Mr. Stormie is in the drawing room with Miss Henrietta, I think, miss."

Ba took a deep breath. "Will you ask Mr. Stormie to step up here, please, Wilson?"

Wilson almost stared. It was out of the ordinary for Ba to ask for one of her brothers, especially in the afternoon. But the maid recovered herself instantly. "Very good, miss. Thank you, miss."

The second after Wilson had closed the door, Ba wished she had bitten her tongue out before she had sent for Stormie. Oh, well, once he arrived, she could contrive some excuse. No, that would be feeble. Now that she had cast the die, she would go through with the results, and when a mildly surprised Stormie stood beside her, she even managed to smile at him.

"Stormie," she said, "I'm dull up here, and Wilson tells me it is such a fine day I feel like an excursion. I wish to join you and Henrietta in the drawing room." She lifted her arms. "Will you carry me downstairs, Stormie?"

Even in her nervous state Ba's alert sense of humor caught the comicalness of the expressions on her brother's and maid's faces.

"Saints have mercy upon us!"

"Well, by Jove, Ba!" Stormie's exclamation sounded as though the words had been jolted out of him. Instinctively he put out a hand to touch her forehead, and then threw Wilson a look of utter bafflement. "Ba, hadn't we better wait—wait for Papa's consent?"

Ba giggled. "But I want to surprise Papa! Dr. Chambers approves. In fact he has been urging me to do this for a fortnight or more. Wilson will vouch for that."

"Yes, it's the truth, sir," Wilson corroborated her mistress in a rather shaky voice.

Stormie drew a deep, slow breath. "Well, by Jove. It'll be a pleasure, Ba!"

He gathered the small figure easily into his arms. His sister clung to him and burrowed her face in his shoulder as he started across the room. There were two flights of stairs. Lengthy ones, and each downward step seemed to jar her from head to foot. It seemed like eternity before Stormie reached a level floor once more. And then the journey was accomplished and her brother had deposited her gently in a great chair. She opened her eyes to see Arabel and Henrietta on either side, wide-eyed and fluttering, and Wilson hovering in the background. As her momentary dizziness passed, she noticed that Stormie was grinning as though he was enormously pleased with himself. Ba could understand the sensation. She had a little glow of satisfaction herself. And then, at the sight of her sisters' perturbed faces, she extended her hands and laughed.

"Well, my dears, you see I have successfully accomplished my great adventure!"

The next day she dispatched a letter to Hatcham. She filled all of three pages with everyday, airy matters, and then used a postscript for her real message.

Instead of writing this note to you yesterday, as should have been, I went down stairs—or rather was carried—and am not the worse.

*B*Y mid-July the changes in Ba were too obvious to be ignored. And Ba's protests that she always gained this way in summer sounded unconvincing; her family and friends remembered that only the summer before she had been so weak and easily upset that even being carried from one bedroom to another had made her faint.

Arabel and Henrietta were awed and rapturous by turns. One after another her brothers exclaimed. Miss Mitford was startled. Mr. Kenyon beamed. And Aunt Jane Hedley (whose arrival in London had so upset the schedule of Mr. Browning's visits) frankly marveled each time she visited 50 Wimpole Street.

"Ba, my lamb, when you left us at Torquay, I said to

your uncle, 'Mr. Hedley, our poor Ba is traveling on her deathbed!' And whenever I've come up to London I've found you in little better case. But now your tide certainly has turned! What does your father say? I warrant he's overjoyed?"

Ba looked away from her aunt's kindly, eager face. She reached out to her little table and toyed with one of Mr. Browning's latest flowers, a dainty, spicy carnation. Aunt Jane's question about Papa made her feel as if she had been touched by someone with chilly fingers. Of all the people around her, she had expected Papa to be the first to see any difference in her and to be the quickest to be glad at her new strength. But Papa was either unaware or unimpressed.

There was a long minute when she could almost feel the silence in the sepia room. Finally, still without looking at Mrs. Hedley, she confessed, "Dear Papa—hasn't said—anything." She stumbled over the words.

"What? What?" Aunt Jane's voice was incredulous. Her crisp silk rustled with her indignant movement. "But you are the darling of his eye, his most precious possession—"

Henrietta's voice was brittle. "Just the same, Aunt, she is quite right. Papa hasn't spoken one single word of pleasure or hope or encouragement to Ba in the month since the rest of us have observed her improvement."

More silence. Flush jumped into her lap and licked her chin. Then Aunt Jane said with the gentle casualness which usually meant she was girding herself for battle in some good cause, "Oh, so he hasn't noticed? It is possible

—yes, he is at an age when he may easily need spectacles. That's a matter which mustn't be neglected. I shall speak to him myself. Oh, you needn't look so perturbed, my dears. I know when to move tactfully."

When Aunt Jane's face wore this particular look of innocence and her voice was as smooth as cream, the Barretts never knew whether she was being completely literal, or if what she said had a cryptic meaning.

But three days later Ba knew. And when Mr. Browning arrived she was quivering under the impact of the astounding, unbelievable tidings which she had heard from Mrs. Hedley barely an hour before.

Mr. Browning had brought Miss Barrett a half-dozen of the poems he had written for his new book. He was beginning to rely on her suggestions, and he had really been anticipating her gay enthusiasm and pointed criticism. But today Miss Barrett's interest seemed at low ebb and her comments were such aimless ones that Mr. Browning pushed the manuscript aside.

"Miss Barrett, do my poems bore you?" he asked pointedly.

Ba blushed furiously, and shook her head in vehement denial.

"Oh, no, no! You must have wondered at me for being in such a maze today. But you see I was told something this noon that seems to have shaken my thoughts all together."

"Not ill news, I hope?" Mr. Browning's expressive face was all concern.

"Most people wouldn't judge it so." Ba's lips curved in

a half-rueful smile. "I heard today that Papa and my aunt are discussing the question of sending me off either to Alexandria or Malta for the winter." She gave him the news in a little rush of words. "Oh, it is passing talk, I dare say. Once I would have been delighted to see such places, but now—there are reasons—" her voice dropped to the merest thread of a sound, "reasons why I'd just as lief be in Wimpole Street even though I am in durance vile during winter."

"Alexandria." Mr. Browning inclined his head thoughtfully. "Well, and may I not as easily ask leave to come 'tomorrow at the muezzin' as next Wednesday at three?" His voice was half-teasing, but it held another quality which made Ba's eyes waver and left her cheeks hot again.

"It would not be, in any case, until September or October, and I shouldn't be consulted. But I would like to see your new book, so let's have the *Bells* ring out before the summer ends."

There! His poetry was a nice, safe, impersonal excuse for her desire to stay in Wimpole Street, wasn't it?

But the forthright Mr. Browning saw no reason for safe, impersonal excuses. He laughed at her, a quick joyous peal. "My book would follow you to Malta or Alexandria —or to the Sahara—in my hands. You won't escape us just by retreating from England. I know how to travel too, you know." Then suddenly the banter dropped out of his voice. "But seriously, I am delighted to hear this news. It means you will sail out of the reach of London's cold and smoke and east winds to places made of sunshine, and

win a full victory over your illness. And you will return
sound and strong and ready to outstrip us all."

Listening to Mr. Browning, Ba really believed he was a
good prophet. She would go to Alexandria. She could, and
she would, be well and strong and upright again. She
began to laugh and to ask Mr. Browning's advice about
the preparations she ought to make for the voyage.

But midnight was no worse for Cinderella than five
o'clock was for Ba. For five o'clock was the hour when
Robert Browning left her; and fifteen minutes after his
departure all the conviction and enthusiasm and delight
which Ba had caught from him ebbed away. A sharp
premonition of disappointment swirled down upon her in
much the same way that sinister thunderclouds were curling over the London sky.

She watched the oncoming storm and its darting thrusts
of lightning with increasing nervousness, resisting the
temptation to ask Wilson to pull the curtains. Did Mr.
Browning mind traveling through a city-shaking storm?
Probably not. He was too assured a person to be even
startled. He would be like Papa, who strode out into the
open to observe storms. But Ba, once Ba had seen a tree
struck at Hope End. The whole trunk was peeled bare in
one fiery second, and up the white inner bark had run a
rose streak, the finger mark of the lightning. The experience had left her "possessed" during thunderstorms, and
it seemed to her to be an ominous sign for a storm to strike
London on this particular day.

Flush, always a little bundle of fear during a thunder-
shower, scurried to the sofa, catapulted upon his mistress

and huddled, whimpering and shivering, in the haven of her arms. Looking down into his terror-filled eyes, Ba struggled to control her own fear.

"It's all right, Flushie! All right! Miss Barrett will hold him fast and no lightning will come after him here. Let's forget the old storm and talk of some good news Miss Barrett heard today. Would Flush like to go traveling? Not just out in the carriage around the park, but on a real voyage like the ones Mr. Browning describes? Miss Barrett thinks she is going to Alexandria, and of course Flush will be going with her."

But even as she talked, Miss Barrett had a return of her qualms. She had been sure, so very sure, while Mr. Browning was with her. His buoyant conviction was contagious. But there was one factor which he didn't know. He didn't know Papa.

The worst of the storm by-passed the Barrett section of London, leaving the July night heavy and damp, and Ba restless and headachy in consequence. It was a poor moment for Mr. Barrett and Aunt Jane to visit her, but they did so directly after dinner. Mr. Barrett caught the uneasy signs in his daughter's face and made solicitous sounds as he tipped her head back.

"My poor suffering darling, you are not a bit well tonight. Have you had visitors today who overstayed their time or excited you?"

"It was the storm." Ba side-stepped Papa's question and told the truth at the same time. "I know you call it disgraceful, Papa, but I always am shaky after a thunderstorm, although—" and Aunt Jane Hedley thought her fleet half-smile, half-grimace had a rather pixie-like quality, "today I did have the grace not to behave like an ostrich."

Mr. Barrett's retort might have been an attempt at humor. "Quite an accomplishment, my dear." He looked toward his sister-in-law. "I happened in here a fortnight or so ago and discovered Ba cowering on the sofa, shutting out the glorious display of lightning with a pillow over her head. And I informed her it was a disgrace to anyone who had learned the alphabet. Well, Ba," the more gentle tone he reserved for his favorite child crept into his voice, "your Aunt Jane has been endeavoring to persuade me that something has been happening to you of which your doting and watchful father has been unaware."

Indeed it had been happening. Her father's casual words were perilously near the truth. Mr. Barrett's crisp voice went on. "She is convinced that you are actually on the road to being well. Do you have the same opinion?"

Ba's eyes were suddenly wistful. She shook her head ruefully. "I do think I am considerably better and stronger, but it is merely my usual summer reprieve. At the first signal of winter—"

"You may be entirely right about the winter!" Aunt Jane broke in vigorously. "All the more reason to get you away! But this is not your usual summer reprieve, Lamb. I saw you last summer, remember, and you were not half so bright. How any of you country-born Barretts survive a London winter is beyond me. And it's past reason to expect that you could be even half-well here. Now that something has turned your tide it would be wicked to risk

it. Go away to Malta or Alexandria and I guarantee you'll
come back blooming."

"Are you longing for a chance to bloom, Ba?"

Ba managed to hold herself quiet. Sometimes Papa took
the most innocent-sounding phrase and seemed to warp
the words. She answered carefully. "You know no miracle
would make me bloom, Papa, but it would be pleasant not
to be coughing and weak all winter. Yes—" she met his
look bravely. "I think I would like to try it, Papa." There,
it was out! She had spoken out on her own behalf, as she
had promised Mr. Browning she would. Now she
searched her father's face anxiously.

Mr. Barrett looked neither pleased nor angry nor surprised. He could be perfectly expressionless and give no
inkling as to whether he was going to thunder a stunning
No or give his benign approval. His only response to Ba
was to fit the finger tips of his right hand carefully and
exactly to the finger tips of his left, and to observe them
closely.

"You see, Mr. Barrett?" cried Aunt Jane triumphantly.
"You see! Ba does desire to go!"

Papa raised his eyebrows and gave his daughter a half-
smile. "Crossing the channel can be very unpleasant, my
dear. One gets seasick, you know. Very ill indeed. And of
course neither I nor Dr. Chambers would be there to care
for you if you were ill either on the voyage or after you
reached your destination, for I cannot and will not desert
my family for any reason whatever. However, if you per-
sist in setting your heart on going, something may be
arranged. One of your brothers and a sister can accom-

pany you. If you actually desire to leave your home and be separated from your doting father for months, why, we must give it every consideration. I will not decide hastily, and you will think it over from every angle, and if you find you choose to stay home, where you have loving care, comfort, and attention, you have simply to say the word. And now, my dear, good night." Mr. Barrett rose and bent to kiss his daughter tenderly. "Come, Jane, Ba is too tired to bear any more talking tonight."

Indeed Ba was tired, so tired that her eyes had begun to play her tricks. It almost seemed as if she saw Wilson make a movement suspiciously like shaking her fist at the closing door. But of course Wilson was much too well-trained to think of anything so improper, although there was no denying that Ba heard her murmuring indignantly, "A good night indeed! As if it could be a good night for my lady!"

But if Mr. Barrett was evasive about the proposed voyage, he was the exception. Ba's brother George was bold enough to volunteer immediately to take her wherever she wanted to go; Arabel was frankly joyous at the prospect. Mr. Kenyon went about chortling happily, and Dr. Chambers gave his official approval in vigorous terms.

"To be sure you must go! Why, yes, you may be seasick, but the lasting benefits would cancel the seasickness over and over again. Go by all means. You may tell Mr. Barrett I order it."

And Ba, who confessed that she had such a terror of doctors that she would rather be ill than be cured by their attentions, had a curious feeling of lightness. A doctor's visit might have its compensations after all, she confided to Robert Browning one afternoon in early September.

Mr. Browning applauded. "Surely, after this report, there will be no more delay? You will be engaging your passage immediately. And when I know your plans, I will submit my own to you. Have you spoken to your father or will Dr. Chambers do that?" His face was alight with eagerness and expectation, but Ba's suddenly sobered.

"No, not Dr. Chambers—I did it." She turned her head away, but Mr. Browning saw the taut lines about her mouth, and felt a tightening of his own muscles. He waited in silence, but when Ba hesitated, he ventured to prod gently. "And—"

Her eyes came back to his, and at their look of baffled desperation and appeal he reached over and covered her twisting fingers with his lean brown ones. "Surely your father didn't say no—not after such positive orders?"

"No, oh, no! He—he didn't say anything!" Ba was making a valiant effort to hold her voice steady, but it dropped to the barest thread of sound, and her fingers made a convulsive movement before they relaxed under the comfort of the Browning clasp. "That's just it. He didn't say anything—except what he's been saying these past two months. 'When the proper time arrives, we shall see.' "

Something in her visitor's voice or perhaps in his clear eyes gave Ba the sensation he was steadying her. "And 'when the proper time comes,' I trust you will see your— dare I say duty—in this affair as everyone else sees it, and go?"

Indeed it did seem as if everyone else was speaking of this voyage as Ba's duty. A duty to her family, her poetry, and herself, to go in quest of the health which was forever eluding her in England. Mr. Kenyon talked to Mr. Barrett in no uncertain terms and then urged Ba to carry through on her own responsibility if necessary; Aunt Jane said the same thing. Her brother George pledged her his services whenever she said the word, and even Arabel told her sister that if only she would go, nothing could prevent Arabel from accompanying her.

It began to seem to Ba as if the whole world was tuned to the rhythm and sound of the one word *Pisa.* (Malta and Alexandria had been vetoed in favor of one of Mr. Browning's favorite cities.)

"Pisa!" chattered Henrietta from morning till night. "Pisa," Arabel murmured in awe. "When you get to Pisa," Aunt Jane would say confidently. "Pisa, yes, a beautiful city," Mr. Kenyon told her wistfully. Even Wilson asked if they were likely to have decent food in Pisa. The birds in the park and the wheels of the carriages on Wimpole Street echoed the syllables. And amid all the talk of Pisa, Pisa, Pisa, there was Papa's dead silence.

"But you will hold fast to your determination?" Mr. Browning pleaded one day when Ba told him she thought the stars were all holding out their dark lanterns against her. "You will not fail us now?"

Ba thought of her brother George's blunt talk with her the night before, when he had urged her to let him engage their passage on the first available boat. It wouldn't matter to Papa whether she went to Pisa or stayed in Wimpole

Street. The very fact that she had said she wanted to go had aggrieved him. That she was willing to be separated from him had made him angry. He would be displeased whether she persisted in going or gave up and stayed in London. The one difference would be that she would take or lose the chance to get really well. So then—?

Ba's chin was resolute when she answered Mr. Browning.

"Oh, I will hold fast. Both George and I will speak to Papa and get a clear answer. And I must do it soon—and I will!"

All the blitheness and enthusiasm with which Mr. Browning usually talked about Miss Barrett's trip to Italy had vanished. Instead he looked grim. "If I only had the right to transport you quietly to Pisa and save you all worry," he said with low vehemence.

The old uneasy feeling in her throat woke Ba the next morning, a sure sign an east wind was blowing. Wilson was lighting a fire. The windows were closed. This was the last week of September. October might be a month of grace, but it might see the coming of an early winter. And she knew from bitter experience what winter meant for her. Papa must speak now!

Her breakfast choked her, her head ached so that she thought it would split in half. If she looked half as sick as she felt it was a most unpropitious time to appeal to Papa, but when she had pushed her breakfast tray away, she nerved herself to ask Wilson if her father happened to be in the house. Wilson somewhat dourly admitted that he was.

"Will you—will you please ask him if it will be convenient to stop in here sometime this morning?" faltered Ba.

"Yes, miss. Very good, Miss Ba," Wilson bobbed dutifully, but her tone implied it might not be good at all.

For ten minutes Ba lay tense, too nervous to open the letters which had arrived with her breakfast, even though one thick envelope was unmistakably from Mr. Browning. And then the steps for which she had been listening approached her door. She dreaded seeing her father's face as he entered, but he was smiling almost genially.

"Well, and how is my pet this wonderful frosty morning? What pretty little blue flowers!" He stopped to admire the latest Browning offering. "I stopped by Moxon's yesterday, Ba, and he tells me he will be putting out a new edition of your poems. And perhaps you'll be getting another volume ready for him this winter?" He pinched her cheek. "Wilson told me you asked for me. It must have been something important for you to send for me in the morning when you know I go out."

Ba wet her lips. "Yes, Papa. I think it's important for me. Papa—won't you tell me if—if I have your permission to go to Pisa for the winter?" At the swift darkening of her father's face, she caught her breath and then plunged desperately on. "I can't wait much longer you know, if I'm really going. Oh, please, please, Papa, don't be upset. I know you said you would answer me at the proper time." Her fingers twisted, and then went out to him imploringly. "But I've got to know—now!"

And then the Barrett silence broke. And all the happiness Ba was to know in other years never quite wiped out the bitter pain of her father's speech that September morning.

"What permission do you expect me to give, you most undutiful daughter? Yes, undutiful and rebellious! You are both, or you would not desire to leave me and tear up our family by carrying one of your brothers and a sister with you. Why should I give my permission? You may do what you like. Indeed, you had better do what you like, for I'm washing my hands of you altogether. Certainly you may go—under my heaviest displeasure!"

Now that it was hopeless, Ba heard herself crying out in indignation, "But why, Papa, why? Why am I undutiful? Dr. Chambers told you the prospects of my health depended upon my escaping the clutches of a London winter. Papa, I—I thought it would be a relief to you to have me better. Won't you tell me why you want me to stay?"

Mr. Barrett was holding himself rigid. "It isn't necessary for me to tell one of my children anything. I know my reasons. But go to Pisa. Once you went to Torquay and kept your brother there against my wishes. Now take another to Pisa! Go your selfish way! You have made all my family rebellious!"

The door slammed, cutting off Ba's anguished cry.

Warned of what had happened in a heartbroken note, an anxious, perturbed, and indignant Robert Browning arrived at Wimpole Street the next Monday. And the Ba he found had swollen eyes and so stricken a face that it was difficult for him to believe she was gallant Miss Barrett whose whole being could be vibrant with intense spirit. Even now she tried to smile as she offered him her cold hands.

"Don't be angry with me," said the tight little voice. "Do not think it was my fault—but I do not go to Italy! It ended as I foresaw. After what you said and Mr. Kenyon and everyone said, and my own deepest convictions, I would go by myself this very hour, but I fall back when I think of my brother and my sister meeting Papa's anger. You do see, don't you?"

Robert Browning saw only too much and too clearly. He had always been very discreet with Miss Barrett, but here was a time to abandon caution. He dropped down beside her sofa and held her in his arms, and in the room which had echoed with her father's angry rage, Mr. Browning's voice sounded very low.

"Be sure, my own, my dearest love, that this is for the best. It is hard to bear now—any other person couldn't bear it—but you will, and you will be well this one winter in London and after this year London winters won't matter to us."

Still dazed by the bitterness of her father's tirade, Ba only half understood him. The only thing that seemed clear in her mind was that she was doomed to her room in Wimpole Street forever. Pisa was "Paradise Lost."

*T*HE whole tantalizing Pisa affair had been a time of agony for Ba. For nearly three months she had had the sensation of stumbling along a treacherous road toward the warmth and strength and freedom which Pisa promised.

Before her sisters and brothers she had been confident and gay, consulting sailing schedules, making eager plans for Arabel. Only to Robert Browning had she let slip her doubts and the increasing torture of her father's silence. Aunt Jane Hedley and Mr. Kenyon thought her almost buoyant. But under everything had run the icy terror of her father's silence. And when he shattered the hope of the Pisa adventure, after the brief thrill of reassuring strength she'd felt this summer, the thought of dropping

back into the endless days of uselessness made her feel as
if she were smothering.

This wasn't the kind of nightmare which dissolved into
something to laugh at with the rising sun. This terror had
the power to touch Ba's brightest days as well as her silent
nights.

But she hadn't reckoned with Mr. Browning. Mr.
Browning had no intention of letting the collapse of the
Pisa plans mean the collapse of Ba Barrett. Until now he
had kept himself restrained, striven to be tact and gentleness itself, but the October day when he found her deso-
late from her father's ungovernable selfishness, all the
Browning barriers went down.

"Never think your father loves you, Ba! You are his
slave. He's proud of your genius, that's all, but he means
to keep a tight hold on it, just for himself. Because he
chooses to give perhaps five minutes or a scant half hour
out of his day to you, he will close the door on your pass-
port to health." All the pent-up anger and indignation
which Robert Browning had barely been able to control
since July broke loose now. "My Ba, it is shocking! You
are in slavery, and I could free you! Oh, Ba, will you let
me teach you how much I love you?"

Nothing in all Ba's life had prepared her for this torrent pouring from Mr. Browning's lips. Later she said it
was like an icy bath, and involuntarily she shrank, eyes
wide. And then the gentle strength of the hands clasping
hers and the understanding in his blue eyes made her
slowly relax. Here was a person of whom she need never
be afraid.

But there could never be any—now be honest, Ba, and use the right word—love between them. That was unthinkable, and Mr. Browning would soon realize it.

She found she could smile at him, at the same time she drew her hands away.

"Oh, my cage is not so bad. Indeed, I think it has been enlarged since you've been visiting it, but you must never say such wild things again, or I must not, I will not, see you again, and you will thank me later in your heart. You will spare me the sadness of breaking off a friendship just when it promises to be a great pleasure to me? Now let's agree to let these things lie and talk of the first of November and the poems which are to come out then. There'll be more poems this winter? You will come to see me through the winter, if you do not decide to go abroad—" Her voice had been carefully light and brave at the beginning, but now suddenly it wavered. "Perhaps that might be better for you? And I would have your letters—"

Mr. Browning tried to look properly grave, but his eyes betrayed him. "I have discovered that I am to have the most urgent business in London this winter," he informed her soberly. "So I will be glad if you will welcome me."

The bitter ending of the Pisa episode touched not only Ba but Arabel and George as well. George was so thoroughly angry that he actually dared to question his father why and how he had refused to let Ba escape a London winter after Dr. Chambers' pointed opinion. Mr. Barrett gave his barrister son a scorching glance and retorted dourly that Ba might go anywhere she pleased, but under

his severest displeasure, and that no child of his had the
right to say "why" to him.

Then he looked down the unhappy group at the dinner
table until his cold glance fell upon the downcast, red-
eyed Arabel. He observed bitterly, "And even my re-
ligiously inclined Arabel has been infected by your
unbecoming behavior. Surely you have learned in church
that it is your duty to submit to the commands of God and
your father? See Ba," he commented with a flourish of his
hand upward toward Ba's room. "She has accepted my de-
cision with good grace and is pleasant and cheerful about
it."

Certainly Ba was behaving in a way that was baffling
to her family. Her anxious sisters and Mr. Kenyon had
expected her to be truly ill, and Aunt Jane had gone into
the sepia room bristling with indignation and fully prepared to find Ba in a dangerously listless state of mind.
But, Aunt Jane confided to her husband afterward, she
had a true shock. Far from being listless, Ba was much
more spirited than she had been in years.

Mr. Kenyon, who had argued with Mr. Barrett long and
boldly on Ba's behalf, was far more distressed and upset
than Ba, and shook his head in bewilderment.

"My dear, from the look of you, one would think disappointment was good medicine!"

"Well, it's bitter enough, and it's been my experience
that all good medicine is bitter," Ba observed wryly. "But
I won't be beaten down again."

Her portly cousin stared at her speculatively through

his thick glasses. He was beginning to wonder about several things.

Possibly the typhoid fever which overtook Occy Barrett that October was a lucky thing for Ba. It wasn't a severe attack but it did distract the family's attentions from Ba when they might have begun asking some embarrassing questions. Mr. Browning scorned the idea that typhoid might be contagious and pressed his urgent business gently but steadily. Ba was too honest a person to pretend she didn't know what the "business" was, although she took almost desperate precautions not to let her family discover this new state of affairs. Once she was shaken with dismay when she almost betrayed it to her father.

He had appeared in her room at a totally unexpected hour one afternoon just as Ba was in the act of pasting Mr. Browning's picture into her copy of "Paracelsus." Stormie and Occy had made too many pointed remarks about that picture for Ba's peace of mind.

"Ah, yes, Mr. Browning." Papa smiled benignly. Like Arabel and Henrietta, he considered Mr. Browning a fine, safe friend for Ba. Completely concerned with poetry!

"It would appear he's as handsome as a poet should be. So you still admire each other, Puss? When was he here last?"

"Yesterday," faltered Ba. She was aghast to hear herself add, "It is strange how Mr. Browning haunts me. I suppose it's because I see so few strangers, but it's really like a persecution."

She could have died after the words were out. If ever

Papa had real reason for alarm it was now! And if he had half a suspicion, the Browning visits would be stopped immediately.

But apparently Mr. Barrett believed Ba to be above all earthly things or too close to her grave to feel human emotion, for he never caught the significance of her remark, and patted her cheek as he retorted with a genial note in his voice, "Now, I think that is being very ungrateful to your friend!"

Ba drew a long breath of relief very cautiously and leaped to a new subject. Did Papa know that Mr. Kenyon had broken his spectacles? Such a shame!

But as to Mr. Browning—she couldn't deny she knew the nature of his "urgent London business" and she was also too forthright to deny to herself that the unthinkable thing had happened. She couldn't deny she loved him.

But she did deny that they could ever be anything more than interested friends. She was sick, a prisoner of weakness, ignorant of everything he knew and loved. He was strong, eager, a person destined to do great things, he must go unburdened by an ailing wife.

So she was weak, he retorted. Well, there was a way for her to gain strength, a way they could take together.

Desperation made him daring. "Oh, Ba," he pleaded one afternoon toward the end of October, "it is not too late even now. See how the summer weather holds! It was made for you to make this adventure. Can't you believe it?"

Ba almost did believe it. Certainly there was something curious about the soft warmth of the air straying in the window—and imagine the windows of the sepia room being open in late October! Had it not been for two or three gold leaves blowing in she would have mistaken the day for midsummer, the sky was so soft, the air so heavenly. A strange impulse roused itself, a quick desire that made her gasp. Not only to be free of her chains of weakness and follow Robert Browning wherever he led, but really to admit that with her, too, admiration and friendship had been swept aside for something else. Looking out at the trees gay with autumn banners, Ba suddenly remembered the warning of her uncle Samuel Barrett long ago. "Ba, beware of loving, for when you do, you will never do it halfway!"

Ba suddenly straightened. No, she couldn't do it halfway. And she did love Robert Browning. She acknowledged it now. She loved him too much to ruin his life by yielding to the temptation he was holding out.

The hands holding hers tightened eagerly. "It is not too late, Ba!" the compelling voice reiterated. "We could be in Pisa within a fortnight."

Ba's gaze came back to the room. Mr. Browning belonged to golden Pisa, but her world was here. She smiled, but she shook her head tiredly.

"Do you know what Mr. Kenyon said to me yesterday in his smiling kindness? 'In ten years you may be strong perhaps—or almost strong.' That's the encouragement of my best friends. What would he say if he knew or guessed? What could he say but that you were—a poet—and I—still worse! He must never know. Please believe that God has put my illness between us—"

"Now that I can never believe!" Robert Browning interrupted soberly. "I have a loving father, so I believe I have a loving God. I'll never believe He made us for each other and led me to find you if He were placing an insurmountable barrier between us. But, if it is your choice, I will wait the ten years for you to grow strong."

"Oh, no, no!" Ba's face filled with distress. Then realizing the implication of what she had said, she caught her breath. "I—I mean I am not right for you! You know I am older—"

Now he was teasing her. "Poor Miss Methuselah! So ancient! Well, I cannot pass for a boy. Bring up your next objection if you please."

A lengthening silence closed between them. As the early autumn dusk began to creep over London, the room itself seemed to take on a more depressed atmosphere. Flush, who had been lying with his nose in the slender path of sunlight while his silken ears were in shadow, suddenly was padding across the floor to his mistress' sofa. He paused long enough to growl at Browning, of whom he had grown intensely jealous, before he leaped into Ba's arms. She scolded him as severely as she had the heart to, glad to hide her face in his thick curls for a moment. Loyal as Ba still was to the father she had thought loved her, she was reluctant to present her greatest obstacle of all to even so understanding a person as Mr. Browning. Flush's bid for attention gave her a minute's respite. But Mr. Browning had a right to know. She bit her lip, then turned toward him, met his gravely inquiring eyes honestly and began to talk softly and rapidly.

"My dear father is a very peculiar person in some matters. There are some things he will not bear. Marriage for any of his children is one. Even my oldest brother suffered on this subject. And once my sister Henrietta had a suitor who dared ask for her hand. My poor sister's knees were made to ring on the floor, and I fainted. You see?"

Mr. Browning's face had grown ominous. He saw very clearly. Robert Browning was the son of a happy home, with a father who loved his wife tenderly and was generous, sympathetic, and understanding, loving his children as human beings and not as goods and chattels. And the thought that brave, winsome, passionately loyal and loving Ba must be under the domination of such a monstrosity as Edward Barrett roused savage instincts which Robert Browning hadn't known he possessed. Then a sudden sinister thought crossed his mind like a sharp pain. Ba started at the rough, harsh sound in his voice.

"And because of your father's insane dictum, will you stay within these four walls forever, forgoing everything your life should be?"

Tears were never easy for Ba, but they rose now and her lips were unsteady, but after a second the dark ringlets shook unhesitatingly. "No. Oh, no! I believe every grown woman has the right to take her own way in this most personal matter, and if I thought I was right, I would not hesitate."

Here was the first break in her defenses, and Browning saw it but he was too wise to pounce upon it. Now he must move with fresh caution for fear of frightening her into retreat.

But the person who finally turned the tide in Browning's favor was one who would have lived the rest of his days in bitter anguish had he known he was responsible. Perhaps Edward Barrett did the best deed of his selfish life when, in order properly to punish Ba for her willful desire to be separated from him, he ceased going to her room for evening prayers. Indeed, he stopped all his visits.

"Cast off entirely," Ba wrote afterward, "and at my side was another. I was driven and I was drawn!"

She had grown up with affection and admiration for her father, but Robert Browning was teaching her ways which Edward Barrett never could know—hope, gentleness, understanding, humor, love, and a promise of real happiness. "We'll go to Italy," he would tell her over and over again, "and stay there for a year or two, and be as happy as day and night are long."

And when she was still gripped by doubts, still held back because of her very love for him, he cried out, "Think of the main fact as ordained by God, will you not, dearest, and not be in doubt ever again?"

But that was the very stone which blocked the road of Ba's thoughts, no matter what paths she took. Ordained by God that Robert Browning of the magnificent destiny should be irrevocably linked with Elizabeth Barrett, who was foredoomed to illness and tragedy? Accept that as Heaven's purpose?

She couldn't explain or argue. Perplexed, distraught, and desperate, her only outlet was in a set of three poems. Poems she did not hand to Browning for criticism. Neither he nor anyone else saw them for several years. She

wrote the first the day after he found her so completely
undone by her father's Pisa tirade:

I have seen thy heart to-day,
  Never open to the crowd,
While to love me aye and aye
  Was the vow as it was vowed
By thine eyes of steadfast gray.

Now I sit alone, alone—
  And the hot tears break and burn,
Now, Belovèd, thou art gone,
  Doubt and terror have their turn.
Is it love that I have known?

I have known some bitter things,—
  Anguish, anger, solitude.
Year by year an evil brings,
  Year by year denies a good;
March winds violate my springs.

I have known how sickness bends,
  I have known how sorrow breaks,—
How quick hopes have sudden ends,
  How the heart thinks till it aches
Of the smile of buried friends.

Last, I have known *thee,* my brave
  Noble thinker, lover, doer!
The best knowledge last I have.
  But thou comest as the thrower
Of fresh flowers upon a grave.

. . . .

Do not blame me if I doubt thee.
  I can call love by its name

When thine arm is wrapt around me;
But even love seems not the same,
When I sit alone, without thee.

And then as her love kept pace with her increasing terror of becoming a blight upon Robert Browning's shining
future, she wrote this desperate cry of "Denial":

I love thee not, I dare not love thee! go
In silence; drop my hand.
If thou seek roses, seek them where they blow
In garden-alleys, not in desert-sand.
Can life and death agree,
That thou shouldst stoop thy song to my complaint?
I cannot love thee. If the word is faint,
Look in my face and see.

I might have loved thee in some former days.
Oh, then, my spirits had leapt
As now they sink, at hearing thy love-praise!
Before these faded cheeks were overwept,
Had this been asked of me,
To love thee with my whole strong heart and head,—
I should have said still . . . yes, but *smiled* and said,
"Look in my face and see!"

But now . . . God sees me, God, who took my heart
And drowned it in life's surge.
In all your wide warm earth I have no part—
A light song overcomes me like a dirge.
Could Love's great harmony
The saints keep step to when their bonds are loose,
Not weigh me down? Am *I* a wife to choose?
Look in my face and see—

And finally, when she could no longer deny to herself
that this terrible and glorious and unbelievable thing

which was happening to her was sweeping everything in her life aside in its relentless surge, she wrote a little poem which betrayed all her feelings:

> There is no one beside thee and no one above thee,
>   Thou standest alone as the nightingale sings!
> And my words that would praise thee are impotent things,
>   For none can express thee though all should approve thee.
> I love thee so, Dear, that I only can love thee.
>
> Say, what can I do for thee? weary thee, grieve thee?
>   Lean on thy shoulder, new burdens to add?
> Weep my tears over thee, making thee sad?
>   Oh, hold me not—love me not! let me retrieve thee.
> I love thee so, Dear, that I only can leave thee.

But that was the one thing it was impossible for Elizabeth Barrett and Robert Browning to do—for either one to forsake the other. And then came the first of the sonnets which were to be her greatest work. It ended on a note of breathless wonder:

>   . . . Straightway I was 'ware,
> So weeping, how a mystic Shape did move
> Behind me, and drew me backward by the hair;
> And a voice said in mastery, while I strove,—
> "Guess now who holds thee?"—"Death," I said. But, there,
> The silver answer rang,—"Not Death, but Love."

But all these poems were Ba's closely guarded secret, and she kept them so for three years. They had not been written easily and she couldn't show them easily, least of all to Robert Browning. At that point in their lives, she could have stood on the floor of Parliament and read them aloud more easily than she could have shown them to Robert Browning.

Almost from the first she had felt he had some power over her and that he meant to use it. She had determined never to see him, and his will had broken down all her defenses. Now there was no escape from the conviction in his face and voice. At length, two months after the Pisa fiasco, all her barricades had crumbled, and she said what must have set all the stars in the universe singing together for Robert Browning.

"Let it be like this, if you will: If I am not ill this winter —and it is almost humanly certain I will be—but if I am not, then, in the time of fine weather, then, not now, I will do whatever you say; but if I am sick, then you will take it as God's will that I do not hamper you."

Now that she had said what he had been patiently awaiting for for many weeks, her words seemed incredible to Browning. And then as incredulity yielded to joy, a slow light filled his face which made Ba blush. But before she hid her eyes in his shoulder her husky voice made one final promise.

"Henceforth I am yours—only not to do you harm."

*N*OW Robert Browning was exultant—as he had good cause to be, for promises were not light things with Ba, and his intuitive understanding of her made him sense that her last words had not been easy ones to say. His arms sheltered her gently, but there was singing jubilation in his voice as he echoed her promise.

"So 'in the time of fine weather if you are not ill'! And you may trust me, my Ba, you will not be ill."

Mr. Browning's glorious confidence always left Ba a little awestruck. A few times she had been lifted on the wave of his buoyancy, but optimism was a quality which did not flourish in the atmosphere of the Barrett house, and possibly Ba had reason for mistrusting it. She smiled a bit wryly now.

"Any day an east wind or a black November frost will prove you wrong. But I'll forgive this November anything because it brings your *Bells and Pomegranates*. You said Moxon promised it for early this month?"

"November 5th—tomorrow." Browning nodded quick agreement. "So toward evening yours will reach you. Why, Ba! What an omen—the first poems of mine which you've helped with your criticisms and suggestions will be published the day after I have your promise. And 'no black November frost' will come to spoil the day."

In his present exalted mood Robert Browning probably wouldn't recognize a frost if it froze the ears off his head, Ba decided; but even a passing white frost, one which merely gave a pleasant zest to London's damp air, could bring on her cough and leave her only the ghost of a voice. And so far Browning had seen only her summer self (an unusually spritely summer self, if he only knew it), although he had never seen her away from the sofa bed. He had yet to meet the feeble, haggard, cough-shaken, useless creature she became when winter took London into its raw, penetrating, and stormy grip. Yes, she had been quite right to bid him wait and accept the verdict of the winter. Not that she doubted him now. She was past having doubts where Robert Browning was concerned, but she was still certain that no one, not even her own sisters, could think of her miserable winter self as anything but a burden. And the winter was so nearly upon them.

Involuntarily she flinched at the thought and Mr. Browning was quick to see the flicker of pain.

"Ba, what is it? Will I ever be able to allay all your doubts?"

Ba's eyes pleaded for understanding. "It was only that all at once I feared your happiness might suffer in the end for having known me." Her words came chokingly. "It isn't distrust of you, but for you—"

Words usually came readily for Robert Browning, but there were occasions when action seemed far more adequate than speech, and this was one of the occasions.

"Oh—" said Ba, gasping when he released her. "Oh!"

True to his prophecy, nothing marred the joy of the day when the seventh issue of *Bells and Pomegranates* appeared, and although she had read and criticized all the poems (but one) as Browning wrote them, Ba pored over the volume for days, commenting eagerly on her favorites.

But there was one very short poem called simply "Song," which Browning hadn't shown her, and she couldn't bring herself to mention it, although her eyes went to it over and over:

> Nay but you, who do not love her,
>   Is she not pure gold, my mistress?
> Holds earth aught—speak truth—above her?
>   Aught like this tress, see, and this tress,
> And this last fairest tress of all,
>   So fair, see, ere I let it fall?
>
> Because you spend your lives in praising;
>   To praise, you search the wide world over;
> Then why not witness, calmly gazing,
>   If earth holds aught—speak truth—above her?
> Above this tress, and this, I touch
>   But cannot praise, I love so much!

But she could and did gleefully repeat all Mr. Kenyon's rhapsodies over the new series of Browning poems. Mr. Kenyon called them "noble, wonderful, of extraordinary power, works of a highly original writer." All these things she could say eagerly and confidently. Browning listened attentively with a dancing light in his eyes. Then he grinned.

"I wish Kenyon were a critic. Ba, you know perfectly well how the reviews are coming in. The *Athenaeum* said 'it is not without talent but spoiled by obscurity and only an imitation of Shelley.' And that was a flattering sample of what the rest said about my 'rubbish.' "

Ba was only too well aware how the critics were treating Mr. Browning's poems. She had been steering the conversation carefully away from the subject all afternoon, but now she nearly leaped upright and actually sputtered in her outburst.

"Oh, the *Athenaeum!* The *Athenaeum* admires only what gods and men reject. It applauds only the mediocre! Dare to breathe a breath above the close, flat conventions of literature, and you are 'put down' to be taught to be like other people. An 'imitation of Shelley'! You! Your poems are made to be remembered and loved when the *Athenaeum* has gone to the winds."

The sparks in Ba's eyes and the faint rose in her cheeks were certainly a new sight. Browning decided that indignation was becoming to Ba.

And although he had more reason now than ever before to wish for a little fame and fortune, Mr. Browning never would be a man to be daunted by a few critics. He knew he was giving his best, and he was honest enough to admit he thought his best was good. Just now he was engaged in something of even more intense importance than his poetry. He was aiding Ba in coming alive and getting well.

As the November days slipped into December, Browning's faith in his and Ba's joint destiny began to seem justified. By some special grace of Providence the wintry weather did not come. All England was marveling at the miracle of the bland season, and even Ba admitted, "The year has forgotten itself into April."

January came in and on the 18th Ba did an unheard-of thing. The thermometer in her room read 68 degrees, a positively balmy temperature for any English house. Ba ordered the startled Wilson to fetch her cloak, and when it was settled around her shoulders, she walked downstairs and into the drawing room.

"Walked, mind!" she reported triumphantly to Browning. "Before, I was carried by one of my brothers, even to the last autumn day when I went out. I never walked a step for fear of the cold in the passages. But yesterday it was so wonderfully warm, and I so strong—it was a feat worthy of the day, and I surprised them all as much as if I had walked out of the window instead."

Browning applauded the news. "That's a far cry from the Ba I knew last May. Do you know I thought you were an incurable cripple from some injury to your spine? But I said you would not be ill this winter. And 'in the time of fine weather—' "

No, Ba wasn't ill. Henrietta and Arabel regarded her with awe; Miss Mitford and Mrs. Jameson were frankly puzzled; perhaps only Wilson and John Kenyon really guessed what was happening. As for Mr. Barrett, he considered himself completely justified in having handled Aunt Hedley's absurd notion about the Pisa expedition exactly the way he had.

"You see?" He gave a rather sour smile at Dr. Chambers' enthusiastic report one late winter afternoon. "There was no need of disrupting our family life by the foolish idea of dispatching her to Malta or Pisa. If she intended to improve she could do it quite as well here in Wimpole Street—of course she will never be well. It obviously has been God's will that she be afflicted for life."

Dr. Chambers snorted. He had no patience with Mr. Barrett's arrogant attitudes.

"Has it occurred to you that the good Lord may have outwitted your stubbornness of last fall by sending Miss Barrett almost as beneficial weather here as she would have found in Pisa?" he demanded loudly, reaching for his hat. "That's a sign of God's will for Miss Barrett, I take it."

Neither of them realized that Ba benefited from something much more potent than the remarkable winter. The mild and sunny weather was the biggest boon she could have had, but coupled with that was the strength and joy she was receiving from the love and determination of Robert Browning.

Even Ba began to believe that she and Browning were living under a miraculous dispensation. She began to talk about the future—about Italy—but she still faltered at giving her definite word.

It really was no wonder that Mr. Browning grew tired, unhappy, headachy, and depressed. So much so that one March day he was too miserable even to give Ba the bouquet of blue violets he had brought her. Perhaps he was unaware when they slipped from his fingers to the soft cushion of the gondola chair.

When he was gone and Ba had eaten her lonely dinner, she moved over to the gondola chair to watch the darting blue and orange flames of the little fire, and Mr. Browning's violets suffered the appalling fate of being sat upon.

It wasn't until the next morning that Wilson, tidying the sepia room, discovered the murdered flowers. "Tsk! Tsk! Why, if I ever! Only see, Miss Ba! Mr. Browning brought flowers yesterday and we never knew." Wilson sorrowfully extended the pathetic evidence. "Only fit for the fire now."

Ba's cry was heartbroken as she caught Wilson's hand. "No! No, let me see!" She cradled the limp blossoms in her hands. "Wilson, fetch me a bowl of water and scissors at once. Oh, Wilson, I—I must have sat upon them—and never knew!"

"Yes, miss," Wilson nodded in mournful agreement. It was useless to bring water for these crushed bits, but if Miss Ba wanted it—

Carefully and lovingly Ba snipped at the broken stems and then dipped stems and heads in water, while the pitying Wilson moved about her work, giving a discouraging backward look every few minutes.

"It's impossible to revive them, Miss Ba," she felt moved

to protest. "They're all crushed and have wanted water all the night. Mr. Browning will bring you more."

With her whole being intent upon her work, a sudden prayer had been pulsing through Ba's heart: If it is meant to be—that I can do him good and not harm—if it is meant that I shall go forth from this place under Robert Browning's guiding hand, let these violets be the sign. If they revive, I will not fail him. . . .

And then Wilson said, "Impossible."

"Yes," Ba said half under her breath. How right Wilson was. Impossible. But still she watched.

An hour later the impossible had happened. The violets had raised their dainty heads and were looking as roguish as though they'd just been snatched from the woods at Hatcham.

Elizabeth Barrett stood up then. Suddenly she felt stronger, more free and eager than she had in her whole life. She had her answer. She, too, had been crushed, had lain in the dark. And, like the violets, she was coming alive. The violets had come from Robert Browning. And so would her future.

*T*HEY knew then that they would marry, and even set a tentative day—the end of the summer. Ba's last doubts went out that March day but her fears remained. Fears of her father's discovery of her love for Robert Browning and their engagement. Forthright Robert Browning had wanted to approach Mr. Barrett, or at least prepare him with a letter. Ba almost collapsed at the thought.

"Oh, no, no! Do you know what would certainly happen? You would be saved the trouble of coming upstairs to my room, for I would be thrown out of the window to you, and you would be welcome to pick up my pieces, put them into a bag, and trot off to Nova Zembla with them!"

Looking at her terrified face and feeling the frightened grip of her small hands, Mr. Browning grimly decided that the sooner Ba was taken out of the reach of the man who could inspire such horror in his favorite child, the better.

"We must tell no one," Ba pleaded. "Mrs. Jameson, Mr. Kenyon—especially not dear Mr. Kenyon, nor my sisters —they must all be able to say 'No, we did not know, we never guessed.' Oh, you must promise."

For a second Browning was perturbed. He was so straightforward a person that to be on his guard every minute with his closest friends, sealing his lips on the thing which would be uppermost in his mind, seemed to him close to deceit, and he was almost ready to be impatient with Ba for asking it. Then perhaps his poet's intuition pricked him, for suddenly he was seeing the sepia room not only as an airless, muted place, but as the place where Ba had lain so long surrounded by luxury—and hopelessness and fear. If he hoped to take her out into sunlight and strength and teach her the joys of living, he could take no risks of touching off her father's unreasoning fury. Robert Browning squared his shoulders and gave his promise.

The dainty French clock on the mantel (there was a clock in the room now) chimed five, and it was time for Ba to ring for Wilson and the coffee tray.

Watching Wilson moving decorously about, and having caught a curious satisfied gleam in the girl's eyes when she answered his greeting, Browning felt a sudden suspicion. His eyes followed the maid as she paused beside Ba's chair to murmur, "Will that be all, miss? . . . Thank you, miss," and retreated noiselessly.

"What of Wilson, Ba?" Mr. Browning thoughtfully stirred his coffee. "You think she doesn't guess? Will it do any good to pretend before her?"

Ba colored. Then she shook her head. "No," she admitted candidly. "Wilson knows, I think. But she would scorn to tell a soul. And in her case it doesn't matter. I have been thinking—" she faltered and Robert Browning looked at her curiously before she finished in a little rush of words, "I have thought of—of taking Wilson with me. For a year, say. She is fond of me, and says she would go anywhere in the world with me. I think she was really disappointed about Italy. And she is very amiable and easily satisfied, and after a year I will be stronger and wiser—"

Miss Barrett was trying to sound casual and self-sufficient, but the amused Mr. Browning could very well guess that the truth was she had never so much as curled her own hair.

He made no effort to restrain his widening grin. Then perhaps he had a vision of Ba struggling with the baffling rites of making a meat pie, and he set down his cup to burst into delighted laughter.

"My dearest, you might go to Pisa without shoes—or feet to wear them—but without your Wilson it would be simply, exactly insane to move a step. I would sooner propose that we live on bread and water and sail in the hold of a merchant ship!"

Mr. Browning's sense of humor came to his rescue fre-

quently in the next months. He rather enjoyed himself
when he found himself sitting beside George Barrett at
someone's dinner, and very courteously inquired, "And
how is your sister, Miss Elizabeth Barrett, these spring
days?" To which George answered gravely, "Reasonably
well, thank you, sir," and both men knew that Mr. Browning could have given much more complete information
about Miss Barrett, having just come from a long afternoon in the sepia room.

Perhaps the people around them weren't quite so deaf
and blind as Ba hoped. At any rate, they could ask some
rather disconcerting questions. George startled his sister
a few days after the dinner by inquiring if she thought of
going to Italy this year.

Yes, she had thought of it, she told him, and was suddenly uncomfortably conscious that she was almost
squirming under his lawyer-like regard. "But there is
plenty of time to do much more thinking."

"I see," said George and Ba felt like a most unsatisfac-
tory witness. She felt still more qualmish when Henrietta
told her later that George had asked her if there was an
engagement between Ba and Mr. Browning.

Mr. Kenyon didn't soothe matters when he observed
with mock mournfulness that there was no use in his coming to Wimpole Street any more now that Robert Browning had taken over the premises.

But the most pointed questions came from shrewd Mrs.
Jameson. That lady settled herself in Ba's room one Au-
gust afternoon for the purpose of offering to take Ba to
Italy, and when her invitation was refused, she set about

probing gently until she could discover what Ba's plans really were.

"Have you given up going to Italy?"

Ba took a deep breath. She wished passionately for Mr. Browning's gay wit and deft way with words. "No, I have not, certainly. Oh, dear Mrs. Jameson, I wish I could be frank, but I can't—not yet."

"But you will go?" If persistence was a high virtue, then Mrs. Jameson certainly possessed the qualifications of a saint. Ba tried to sound extremely matter-of-fact and was a little pleased with the result.

"Yes, if something unforeseen doesn't happen. Do let me give you another cup of coffee." Ba reached for the steaming pot.

"Thank you, it is good." Mrs. Jameson held up her cup, but even as Ba poured, she returned to her attack. "And you will have efficient companionship?"

"Oh, yes!" Ba could answer that one with swift assurance.

Mrs. Jameson absent-mindedly gave Flush a tiny cake to nibble while she considered this last. And then either her real anxiety or her curiosity got the upper hand and she cried impatiently, "But what are you going to do? But oh, I mustn't inquire!"

Which was exactly what Ba thought. She glanced hurriedly at the door. Any minute Arabel and Henrietta would be coming in. Her voice was a little unsteady. "I promise to tell you when everything is settled. I won't be going until the end of September at least, and this time I'm not going to make any premature fuss."

The older woman's eyes filled with amazement and then held swift understanding. "In fact there is only an elopement for you!"

Ba heard herself laughing in a way that would have done credit to Robert Browning himself. She never knew what was said or done after that until Mrs. Jameson stood up to go. "Then she looked and looked into my eyes like a diviner," Ba told Browning the next day, "and she told me that she and her niece would be in Paris during September. That's a good omen for us, isn't it? But dearest," Ba's face was suddenly clouded, "surely nobody will say we've eloped? Nobody will use that word?"

Mr. Browning laughed easily these days. "Let them call it 'felony' or 'burglary' so long as they don't come to church with us and propose my health after breakfast. Who cares?" And then abruptly he was grave. "Ba, let's have it over with very soon now. I have a presentiment that suddenly you will be removed to Devonshire or Sussex, and then our difficulties will be multiplied. And surely you are ready for our great adventure now?"

Was she? Would her strength hold at the last? She had no doubt about her determination, but could she control her physical self, her treacherous nerves? All this spring and summer she had been building up toward what Robert Browning called their "great adventure." She had astonished her sisters not only by going driving but by walking, and paying calls on Mr. Kenyon and "Treppy," an old Creole servant of the family, and visiting Mr. Boyd, the blind Greek scholar with whom she'd read Greek in her girlhood. She had gone shopping for a bonnet and flannel-lined slippers to wear on the stone floors of Pisa; Mr. Kenyon had taken her to see the railway, and she had even gone to Westminster Abbey.

But for all these excursions, when the time really came, could she do what she knew it meant? She could leave Wimpole Street easily enough, and, heartbreaking though it would be, she could leave her family; but could she bring her father's terrible bitter anger down upon her sisters and brothers for suspecting what was happening in his household and not giving him warning? It was so terrible to cause pain for the first time in her life! She gave a long shudder, and then, looking up, she met the intent, questioning eyes of the man beside her, and something in their gaze wrenched a little cry from her.

"Oh, Robert, is it necessary for me to say 'I will not fail you'? Could I? I will not fail!"

The last weeks of August were torture to both impatient Browning and nervous Ba. The house at 50 Wimpole Street was filled to overflowing with relatives. Arabella Hedley and her family were making it their headquarters until Bella's wedding, and while there were Hedleys and Clarkes and Bella's fiancé, Mr. Bevan, darting in and out at all hours, Ba didn't consider it safe for her own fiancé to appear. She had to put up with Mr. Bevan, who talked to her about church architecture by the hour, instead. "And church architecture is not my strong point," she wrote plaintively to Robert. (She called him Robert, now, which was a very daring thing to do. Aunt Jane, for instance, had been married to Uncle Hedley for thirty years and more, and still addressed him as "Mr. Hedley.")

Uncle Hedley, incidentally, was giving Ba some kindly advice. She must stand firm and get to Italy. England certainly would not have another balmy winter. Aunt Jane claimed she would not think of advising, and immediately afterward said emphatically, "But you ought to go, Balamb. To live on in this fashion in this room is lamentable."

It was at that unfortunate moment that Mr. Barrett walked in. Ba felt her heart pounding in her throat. She colored and cringed under his accusing eyes.

"So you're still prattling about going to Italy? I really believe you would enjoy shutting the door on your father's house forever."

Ba opened her lips with an effort, but the only result was a small, wordless exclamation. Aunt Jane turned slightly so that her buxom figure partially shielded her niece from view.

"We were just remarking, Mr. Hedley and I, how well Ba is looking," she said smoothly. "And a winter in Italy, or even with us in Paris, would certainly restore her completely."

Mr. Barrett snorted skeptically. "You think so, do you? Mumpish! That's the way she looks to me. Mumpish!"

Once Ba managed to escape the clatter and confusion of Bella's wedding preparations and drove to St. John's Wood for a calming hour with Mr. Boyd.

When she stood in the doorway of his little, dark, musty room and saw him sitting there in his chair, his chin buried in his chest, looking for all the world like a statue of Neglect, her throat burned with tears. Back at Wimpole

Street she had left a gay young cousin, all joy and eager-ness over her approaching wedding, and she herself had strong hope and deep happiness ahead of her; and here sat Hugh Stuart Boyd, old, blind, neglected, living only with his memories of the long-dead Greek poets. He toler-ated hearing Elizabeth Barrett's poetry for the sake of the girl who had pleased him by reading Greek aloud to him, but he claimed he didn't like it.

Ba went softly into the dingy little room, Flush padding dejectedly after her. She stooped and kissed the old man gently on the forehead, and he moved his head slightly. "Is it Elibet?" (He always said the name "Ba" offended his ears, so he had evolved "Elibet.")

She sat in a low chair, put her hand on the sleeve of the shabby dressing gown, and present-day England and even Robert Browning began to seem very distant as they talked about the Greeks and Cyprus. But gradually the cracked old voice faded and the blind man frowned.

"Elibet, something's happening to you—going to hap-pen. Wait. Let me think. Elibet, never tell me you're going to become a nun!"

It was so surprising a guess that Ba was startled into laughing until the tears ran down her cheeks, and Flush came darting over to her whining with fright. She cud-dled him with her left hand while she gave Mr. Boyd re-assuring pats with the other. "Oh, no, dear friend. How could I? Oh, never!" she managed to gasp between spasms. "Oh, dear Mr. Boyd, whatever made you think that?"

"You're going to make a great change in your life!"

persisted the old man obstinately. "Ha! Wait! I have it now. Elibet, you're going to be married."

How had he guessed? She never knew, but after her betraying quick gasp, there could be no denying it. So in that little room, which was even more dismal than her own, she spoke the name Robert Browning, told of his letters, their meetings, his generous love, and their hopes, and of his genius. Mr. Boyd shook his head stubbornly over the last. "No genius, Elibet. His poetry's too degenerate. But I approve of your marrying him and living in Italy. Let it be soon, and don't let anything prevent it. Have Arabel come tell me about it when you're gone."

New tears came and slid down her cheeks. Everyone was saying go to Italy! Go! Everybody approved and was concerned. Everybody except the one man she had thought would care most of all. Was Robert right? she wondered bitterly. Had her father cared only to possess her because he was proud of her talent? She rose a little stiffly to bid Mr. Boyd good-by. Well, that life was over now. Ahead lay October—and her promise to Robert.

SEPTEMBER did not come in auspiciously. Robert Browning was not well. The weather had been unbearably hot, which made Ba listless and Mr. Barrett look "as though thunder had passed into him." Altogether Ba was not in the right condition to face the calamity which descended on the second day of September.

She and Arabel had been shopping in Vere Street and, as usual, Flush scampered gaily in and out of the shops. Ba knew he was at her heels as she stepped into the carriage—and then he wasn't!

"Flush!" she called. "Come, Flush!" But there was no Flush. "Flush!" She screamed his name this time. There was no cascade of sharp little answering barks.

Arabel had come tripping from the shop, followed by a young clerk bearing their purchases. The world seemed to be falling into a pleasant pattern this afternoon. Dear Ba was certainly getting well, genuinely so, and Arabel strongly suspected she would be going to Italy soon. A number of delightful things had been happening to the Barretts lately—and today Papa had given her funds to buy the goods for new winter gowns for all three sisters.

And then suddenly Arabel heard her sister's frantic cry and her gaiety was extinguished like a candle flame exposed to a strong current.

"Ba, Ba, love! What has happened?" she cried, looking fearfully about her. "Has Flush been struck by a carriage?"

Ba drew a long breath. "No, no! He's gone!"

Arabel raised questioning eyes to the cabby, and the sunburned old man nodded gloomily. "That's about hit, miss," he corroborated mournfully. "I sat here a-dozin', worse luck, so I seed nothin', but there ain't a doubt but that 'the society' has 'im, poor little mite."

The shop clerk glumly agreed with this verdict. "Many's the dog that's been snatched in these streets, a-following his mistress to and fro out of the shops," he informed the sisters. "That society has slippery ducks on the watch. Poor little tyke must have been caught up from under the very wheels—"

Ba had been beating her cold hands in a frenzy of impatience. Now she was interrupting the man in a far sharper tone than Arabel had ever heard from her. "For heaven's sake, Arabel, how can you waste time standing there? My good man, put the boxes in at once! Arabel, we must be off! We must see about doing something!"

Both her sister and the young clerk hurried to obey her commands. Neither Ba nor Arabel needed to ask the two men about the society. Both of them knew about that bold, notorious gang of organized dog thieves which did a thriving business snatching the dogs of wealthy families and extorting a high ransom by threats of torture for the pets.

Twice before had poor Flush been in their hands, and each time Mr. Barrett had been extremely angry with Ba for consenting to pay the ransom. Now, Arabel reflected ruefully, when Ba obviously was under Papa's disapproval, things would be even more difficult. Poor Ba. She stole a look at her sister, sitting rigid in her corner, her eyes blazing in a face so white that Arabel, timid by nature, was really startled. She moved closer to Ba and put a comforting hand over the tense ones.

"Don't look so, Ba!" she implored. "You will frighten Henrietta and Wilson and upset dear Papa so that we shall never be let to drive out alone again. Oh, don't worry, dearest! You will get him back directly for ten pounds at most."

Ba tried to edge away from her sister. "Yes, yes, I know!" she said in that strange sharp voice. "Of course I know! But Flush doesn't, and he will be in despair all this while."

Once they were home she sent Arabel in search of the nearest brother, who happened to be Henry. Henry shrugged over the story, but he promised to do something,

and set off to the unsavory section of London which was
known to be the stronghold of a Mr. Taylor, the captain
of the banditti. On returning home he reported that this
questionable character plainly knew all about Flush, and
promised to let them hear about terms that evening. Nobody came, however, probably because Henry had remarked that Miss Barrett was resolved not to give very
much. Hearing that, Miss Barrett almost stamped her
foot.

"Of course they will make me give what they choose. I
am not going to leave Flush to their mercy, and they
know that as well as I do. My poor Flush!"

It was obvious that nothing more could be done about
his rescue that night. Ba shut herself up in her room and
wrote an anguished letter to Robert.

Wednesday dragged by drearily, with no word from
Flush's captors. At night she had a letter from Robert, but
it did not comfort her.

*Poor Flush—how sorry I am for you, my Ba! But you
will recover him, I dare say . . . not, perhaps directly; the
delay seems to justify their charge at the end: poor fellow
—was he no better than the rest of us, and did all that
barking and fanciful valour spend itself on such enemies
as Mr. Kenyon and myself, leaving only blandness and
waggings of the tail for the man with the bag? I am sure
you are grieved and frightened for our friend and follower, that was to be, at Pisa—will you not write a special
note to tell me when you get him again?*

Ba snatched her pen and the nearest sheet of paper
and wrote a hasty answer.

"Our friend and follower, that was *to be"—is* that, *then,
your opinion of my poor darling Flush's destiny—? I
"shall not recover him directly"* . . . *But, dearest, I am
sure that I* shall. . . . *I knew from the beginning where
to apply and how to persuade. The worst is poor Flush's
fright and suffering. And then, it is inconvenient just now
to pay the ransom for him* . . . *But I must have Flush, you
know* . . . *There is a dreadful tradition in this neighbour-
hood, of a lady* . . . *having her dog's head sent to her in a
parcel. So I say to Henry—"Get Flush back, whatever
you do."*

How could Robert have written so airily? she wondered
as her eyes went toward the empty purple dish.

In the morning Wilson came in with such a distraught
expression on her face that Ba feared the thieves had done
their worst.

No, it wasn't that, praise Heaven, but Wilson's news
was heavy enough. The archfiend Taylor had arrived at
50 Wimpole Street the night before, so Wilson had been
told in the kitchen, with the word that his society would
accept six pounds, six guineas; and he would charge an
extra half guinea for his trouble. Henry Barrett might have
paid, but his father heard the commotion and bade his
son refuse. And also, Wilson reported having heard from
Minnie the housekeeper, he desired Mr. Henry not to tell
Miss Ba a word about it. It was several minutes before Ba
could control herself to request Wilson to fetch Mr.
Henry at once.

That young gentleman did not look very happy when
he finally appeared. He admitted the truth of what Wil-

son had heard, said miserably he was sorry, but Papa—Ba knew Papa.

Ba spoke out now as none of the Barretts had ever dared speak. "Is Flush Papa's dog?" she asked bitterly.

Henry was the picture of distraction. "I know, I know. Oh, Ba, I am so sorry! I would have paid, but Papa forbade—"

His sister went over to him, put hands on his coat lapels, and lifted her pleading eyes. "Go find this man Taylor again. Now! This morning. Take my money with you! Please, Henry, please! I am nearly mad when I think of poor Flush's suffering."

But Henry would not. All he could mumble was, "Papa forbade it."

If only Robert were here!

But Robert, it seemed, was really sick. And as if that wasn't enough, his letter which came in the morning post showed him taking a decidedly cold-blooded attitude. He wrote that the idea of Ba (or any other victim of the unsavory society) paying a ransom for a stolen dog was wrong, weak, and simply an encouragement for the disgraceful system of extortion. Mr. Browning would say to the bearer of a ransom demand, "See?" Whereupon he would give the ten pounds to the first beggar in the street.

Oh, he would, would he? Ba seized her pen and wrote furiously:

Do you mean to say that if the banditti came down on us in Italy and carried me off to the mountains, and, sending to you one of my ears, to show you my probable fate if you did not let them have . . . how much may I venture

to say I am worth? . . . five or six scudi . . . would you
wait, poised upon abstract principles, for the other ear?
. . . Would you, dearest? Because it is as well to know
beforehand, perhaps.

And then compunction seized her, and she added, *Ah*
—how I am teazing you, my beloved, when you are not
well . . . I love you always.

In Hatcham Mr. Browning was having his own re-
grets. He wrote another note late that same day in which
he told Ba that even before he could seal the letter he'd
written in the morning he had become so ill he had been
forced to throw himself on his bed. If he had sounded
cross would she forgive him?

Saturday morning had dawned, and edged its way to
noon, and no Flush. Ba had known there would be no
further move from the thieves, but Mr. Barrett remained
adamant, and Henry continued lukewarm. Slowly resolution formed in Ba. She knew perfectly well what must be
done, and who must do it. Little loving Flush, who had
been her loyal companion for three dark and sad years
before this brighter one dawned, was waiting somewhere
for her to rescue him, and wondering why she didn't
come. He was only a comical bundle of silky hair, a badly
spoiled little dog, but he had been faithful in her times of
need. How could she be less in his?

"Wilson!" she called.

"Yes, miss?"

"Get my cloak, and something for yourself. And then
run downstairs and ask Jemima to fetch a cab."

The affectionate maid's face brightened. Ba had refused to drive since the day when Flush had been snatched. "Yes, miss! The day is that grand. Being out will do you good. Will you be taking Miss Arabel or Miss Henrietta?"

"No, no!" Ba exclaimed hastily, then added, "Miss Henrietta goes to my aunt and Miss Arabel has a meeting with the choir children at the chapel. We will go alone, you and I." She made an effort to smile, and Ba's smile could be captivating. Wilson felt as though Miss Ba had taken her into some great confidence, and her "Very good, Miss Ba!" had almost a singing quality.

Descending the stairs, Ba thought that Wilson would not have sounded so pleased had she known the direction their drive would take. Wilson was a generous, loving soul, but no more courageous than Ba herself.

When the two were settled in the cab, the cabby cocked his head inquiringly, and Wilson asked, "Where to, miss? Around the park or to Mr. Boyd's?"

"No," said Ba a little faintly. Then her spirit rose. She looked the driver in the eye. "Take us to the headquarters of a Mr. Taylor, captain of a dog society. I don't exactly know the direction."

The cabman dropped his jaw and Wilson stared at her mistress with wild eyes. "Mercy upon us!"

The driver, a burly, clumsy-looking fellow, but with kindly, honest eyes, surveyed his two fares dubiously. Such a little, dainty lady to give such a command. "Ye mean it?" he asked, as though he hoped his ears had played him tricks. He had driven Miss Barrett and her sisters around the park or to the shops many times. Indeed he knew all the decorous and circumspect drives Miss Barrett undertook, and more than once had been warned by her sisters or Wilson to drive easily and carefully, since Miss Barrett was an invalid and very timid.

"Yes," said the timid little invalid.

It was not for Wilson to protest Miss Ba's commands, but the thought of her lady deliberately setting out for a den of London's most notorious thieves drove poor Wilson to desperation. "Oh, Miss Ba, please! You mustn't! Ask Mr. Alfred or Mr. Occy."

Ba shook her head with stubborn weariness. Not one of her brothers would stir for fear of Papa's condemnation.

The cabby made a clucking noise with his tongue. He remembered now the gossip he'd been hearing of how the famous Miss Barrett's wee dog had been stolen. And so the men of her family wouldn't go and bargain with the society? He touched his cap respectfully.

"I'll take ye there and back again safely, miss. Safely as I would me own daughter. But I'll be askin' ye this." Sincere anxiety sounded in the gruff voice. "Ye won't be gettin' out of me cab?"

"Oh, no!" Ba breathed fervently.

So they set off into a section of London which the sheltered Miss Barrett had never even suspected existed. Such unsavory streets and mean houses, and the people —Ba cringed as they passed the inhabitants of the district. Not because they were ragged or filthy (as some of them undeniably were), but because for the first time in

her life Ba saw evil staring at her from a human being's
face. Wilson, aware of the sinister things which might
happen if her mistress was recognized, was perilously
close to tears.

Eventually the cabby had to stop at a pub to ask his way,
and out came three or four men who nodded wisely and
informed Ba, "Yes, you want Mr. Taylor, ma'am!"

Summoning all her courage, Ba folded her shaking
hands and inclined her head. Yes, she had heard that was
the gentleman's name. Almost instantly the cab was surrounded by a crowd of the most unprepossessing speci-
mens Ba had ever seen. One boy had run ahead to a
certain house and now came back to say that Mr. Taylor
wasn't home, but wouldn't the lady get out and wait?

A negative growl came from the cabby, and Ba shook
her head emphatically. Well, then, she should see Mrs.
Taylor. The boy, who evidently acted as a messenger,
sped away again and returned shortly escorting the most
enormously fat woman Ba had ever beheld. She informed
Ba that her husband might be back in a few minutes, or
in so many hours, and asked if she wouldn't like to get
out and wait?

The crowd nodded and yelled approval, even trying to
open the cab door. Wilson shrieked and clutched her
mistress' gown.

"As you value your life, miss, don't budge from this
seat! We'll be murdered for certain if you do!"

Denials of any such intentions rent the air. Oh, no! The
gang about the cab lived but to oblige the little lady! So
help them!

Miss Elizabeth Barrett had never been been faced with a situation like this, but not for nothing was she the daughter of some of the proudest families of England and Jamaica. Queen Victoria herself could not have excelled Miss Barrett in dignity at that moment as she returned the feminine bandit's smirk with a cool look of authority.

"No, it will not be necessary, thank you, for me to get out; but it is necessary that Mr. Taylor should keep his promise about the restoration of a dog he agreed to restore. I beg you to induce him to come to Wimpole Street today, and not defer it any longer."

Wilson gasped; so did the excited gang around the cab. People usually did not address either Taylor in this peremptory fashion.

Mrs. Taylor stared, and then she was all gracious smiles. "Yes, certainly I do believe that Mr. Taylor has left home on that very business." She poised her head first to the right and then to the left with what she considered easy grace. "He will give it his very best attention."

"Of course!" the gang assured them with parrot-like chorus. "Anything to oblige the little lady!" In the midst of all this politeness the cabby took a hand in affairs and cracked his whip.

Bringing his cab to a standstill before 50 Wimpole Street, the cabby appeared relieved that their dubious mission was accomplished. "Here you be, miss. And if I may make so bold as to say so, you're a brave 'un."

The Captain of the society did appear later, and promised to return Flush immediately for a payment of six guineas. Ba sent Occy down with the money, and all would have gone smoothly if Alfred Barrett hadn't walked into the house at that inopportune moment and heard the transaction. He promptly reacted in a typical Barrett manner, losing his temper, and shouting to Taylor that he was a swindler, a liar, and a thief. Naturally this was more than the insulted Mr. Taylor could stomach, and he in turn shouted that no gentleman was spoken to in such language, and that Flush would never enter the Barrett door again. Nor would he. He flung down the six guineas and hurled himself out of the house.

To use Ba's own words, there "followed a great storm." Henrietta and Arabel were in frightened tears. Occy was bitterly angry and more than a little disgusted at the wrecking of his negotiations and flailed his brother with uncomplimentary names.

"Just as I was in the act of restoring Flush to poor Ba you must needs come in and yell insults at the man Ba and Henry and I have been trying to placate—"

Alfred stood against the drawing room door, his arms folded, head flung back coolly. "How can you insult a man by speaking the truth?" he asked mockingly.

There was so much commotion and confusion that none of the harried Barretts saw Ba coming downstairs—Ba, who had never been known to make the journey down the two long flights twice in one day. She confronted Alfred with blazing eyes.

"So, just for the satisfaction of trying on names which fit, you risk my dog's life!" Her voice shook with anger, but its very softness gave it a compelling quality against her brothers' upraised ones. "And now you force me into going to seek this bandit once more. Will you come with me to undo your mischief?"

Was this Ba, the gentle, timid, sick little sister they had known for so many years? The Barretts had the sensation that their world was being turned upside down.

"Papa!" sobbed Henrietta, longing for that parent for the first time in her life. "If dear Papa were only here, all of you would behave!"

And that morning Henrietta had been dancing a polka by herself because Papa had betaken himself to the country for the day. Alfred, however, appeared capable of filling his father's place. He favored Ba with a look of cold disapproval. "I think you are quite mad," he informed her. "No dog is worth a ransom."

A slim young figure interposed itself between the arrogant Alfred and the trembling Ba. Sette, the seventh Barrett brother, grinned slightly as he pushed Alfred aside, but his voice was gentle, and so was the arm he put around his sister's waist.

"Dash it all, Ba, let me get you to your room, and I swear I'll go and redeem Flush myself. Instantly!"

Ba was suddenly so undone that Sette ended by helping her upstairs. She was too weary to speak, but she obstinately refused to go to bed. It was now or never for Flush. She strained her ears. Would the sound she was waiting for ever come? And then—was there really a sound, a padding of tiny feet? Her head and Wilson's jerked up at the same time. Wilson was at the door, and Flush, thin and dirty beyond description, came in, and rushed straight to his purple dish.

"DOVER — Reigate — Tun-
bridge—" Henrietta's crimson and blue flounces fairly
sang as she whirled before her sister's startled eyes. "Our
benevolent Papa says we may decide among us." She
made an exaggerated curtsy, and the impish dancing of
her dark eyes belied her demure expression. "Well, Ba,
what do you say—Tunbridge—Reigate—Dover?"

Ba looked wildly around the group of her brothers and
sisters assembled in the drawing room. Alfred and Sette
were standing together, watching her with expectant
grins; George rested one arm upon the marble mantel
while he surveyed Henrietta's performance with pursed
lips. Henrietta had been doing her impromptu polka
alone, but now Occy caught her hands and they went
whirling and laughing down the length of the drawing

room together until to Ba everything seemed like a gigantic wheel of distorted colors and sounds. She gripped the arms of her easy chair and gasped for breath. It was Arabel's soft, quick voice and gentle touch on her forehead which made the chaos begin to subside.

"Henrietta! Occy! Stop! Can't you see what you're doing to Ba? She's sheet white! Dearest, Henrietta hasn't gone quite mad, it's only that Papa sent Alfred home with such extraordinary news."

"Extraordinary!" exclaimed the irrepressible Henrietta, "stupendous—petrifying!"

Arabel turned her shoulder. "Perhaps we should have broken it to you by gentle degrees, but Henrietta was seized with the idea that we should all enjoy it together. I think now she wanted to explode it in your lap like a bomb." She stroked her sister's hair back from the damp forehead. "From the way Henrietta burst out you couldn't have had the least notion of what she was talking about. But it's a delightful thing, I assure you it is, dearest."

Oh, was it? Despite Arabel's happy smile and reassuring tone, Ba sat like a statue. Henrietta's very mention of towns had waked the echo of Robert's premonition that she would be taken to Devonshire or Sussex "and then our difficulties will be increased!"

"Tell her calmly, now, Henrietta," Arabel was saying.

Calmness was still beyond Henrietta. She laughed and her cheeks blazed with excitement, but her words, though they came out in a torrent, were intelligible enough.

"Well, Ba, this night an edict has gone forth, and George is to go tomorrow to take a house at Dover, Reigate or Tunbridge. Dear Papa was so gracious as to say it did not matter which, only he must have this house empty for a month to have it cleaned and repaired! Oh, Ba, won't it be glorious to be out of this stuffy old hole for a whole month?"

"Lay your plans for much longer," Alfred interjected wisely. "There's much more than a month's work here, what with painting and papering. A good six months' respite from Wimpole Street, mark my word."

"And we may decide!" Henrietta was clapping her hands and chortling, and then suddenly the unresponsiveness in Ba's face struck home. "Why, Ba dearest," she faltered in surprise. "Aren't you glad? Aren't you even pleased?"

Pleased? Glad? Ba was frightened as she had never been frightened by storms or illness or even by Bro's disappearance. She opened her lips and spoke in a strange, tight voice.

"Glad? Why should I be? It is not at all for my sake that we go. If I had been considered, we should have been taken away much earlier, certainly not now, when the cold season is at hand. I have no opinion as to places."

Alfred chuckled in the embarrassing silence. "I can guess why our Ba isn't happy!" He flung himself on a nearby sofa. "No poet to come spend long afternoons at Reigate. Don't you think Mr. Browning could find his way to Reigate, Ba? You'd better cheer up, he's really quite a famous traveler, you know."

George looked a little abashed, and came over to pat Ba's shoulder awkwardly.

"I'm only going to look in Reigate first, Ba," he said. "I think it is quite likely, yes, entirely probable—" he spoke with such ponderous reassurance that at any other time Ba would have been amused, "that I will find the houses there thoroughly unsuitable. And as to your friend, Mr. Browning, I will say that I have found him a most estimable man, quite frank and open. I doubt if he will forget you while we are out of London."

A ghost of a smile crossed Ba's face as she thanked him in a small voice.

The Barretts had only one topic of conversation at dinner, but Ba was mute. She had no appetite, and as everyone knew her dislike of desserts, it was easy enough for her to slip away from dinner early.

It was a hot night, that 10th of September, but Ba's hands were cold as she sank into the gondola chair and reached for her writing desk.

Dearest, you are a prophet, I suppose . . . This night, an edict has gone out . . ." she raced on to tell it exactly as Henrietta had told it to her.

Now!—what can be done? . . . Decide, after thinking. I am embarrassed to the utmost degree, as to the best path to take. If we are taken away on Monday . . . what then? . . . Therefore decide! It seems quite too soon and too sudden for us to set out on our Italian adventure now—and perhaps even we could not compass—

Well—but you must think for both of us . . . I have just a moment to seal this and entrust it to Henrietta for the morning's post.

> *More than ever beloved, I am your own BA.*

And now Ba had an odd sensation of strength and soaring exultation. At the bottom of the sheet she wrote a single line which canceled all her doubts and hesitations. *I will do as you wish—understand.*

Certainly Robert Browning understood. The double shock contained in Ba's short note swept every vestige of illness out of his body. He sent an equally brief, feverish missive to Wimpole Street, dated 12 o'clock Thursday.

"I will do as you wish—understand"—then I understand you are in earnest. If you do go on Monday, *our marriage will be impossible for another year—the misery! You see what we have gained by waiting. We must be* married directly *and go to Italy. I will go for a license today and we can be married on Saturday. I will call tomorrow at 3 and arrange everything with you. We can leave from Dover &c., after that,—but otherwise, impossible! Inclose the ring, or a substitute—I have not a minute to spare for the post.*

Ever your own R.

At three o'clock on Friday, Robert Browning was ushered for the ninetieth (and last) time into the sepia room, and for the first time in their acquaintance, he was the more nervous of the two. No poise nor calm about him now. He nearly stepped on Flush, wasn't aware of Wilson's presence, and sat tensely on the edge of the gondola chair giving Ba orders in swift, staccato sentences.

"You will come to St. Marylebone Church at quarter to eleven tomorrow morning—better still, ten-thirty. Bring Wilson, of course. I will make the arrangements with my friend."

Ba buried her face in his coat. "Oh, Robert, ask your mother to forgive me, will you? If I were not there, she could be! It is a great grief to me never to have known her or your kind father and dear sister."

The relationship between Robert and his mother was a rich and tender one. It must have given him a sharp pang to think she could not be present at this important moment. Perhaps the fact that he didn't answer Ba showed how deep his hurt was, for his voice wasn't steady as he hurried on.

"And the marriage over, you can take advantage of circumstances and go early or late in the week. Your own packing won't seem strange in the light of the family's exodus. Write short notes to the proper persons, promising longer ones, if necessary."

There was no denying it, Robert was a very nervous bridegroom.

His visit was short and soon over. There was the license to get—no, he hadn't gone for it yesterday after all—and the ring to buy, and the minister to see, and he must write a note to the friend who would stand up with him.

With all these details on his hands, the day must have gone rapidly enough for Robert, but for Ba it crawled like a lame snail. She couldn't read, she couldn't write, even her words stuck in her throat until Arabel regarded her with such a grave and suspicious look that Ba had a wild conviction her thoughts must have grown transparent.

Ba finally busied herself tying Robert's letters together in little packets. Then she gathered together her infinitely

secret sonnets. One fluttered to the floor and as she re-
trieved it, the words leaped up at her.

> If I leave all for thee, wilt thou exchange
> And be all to me? Shall I never miss
> Home-talk and blessing and the common kiss
> That comes to each in turn, nor count it strange,
> When I look up, to drop on a new range
> Of walls and floors, another home than this?
> Nay, wilt thou fill that place by me which is
> Filled by dead eyes too tender to know change?
> That's hardest. If to conquer love, has tried,
> To conquer grief, tries more, as all things prove;
> For grief indeed is love and grief beside.
> Alas, I have grieved so I am hard to love.
> Yet love me—wilt thou? Open thine heart wide,
> And fold within the wet wings of thy dove.

She touched the words softly before she slid the paper
in its proper place. These last few weeks when Robert
had been ill or otherwise hindered from coming had
taught her the answer to her questions. She might miss
"the home-talk and the common kiss," but not only would
he be all to her, he was already the part of her life she
couldn't cast off, couldn't forgo, closer than breathing
itself. And what was her portion to be? What had she to
give him in return? For many months she had thought
she must always stand empty-handed, but now she found
the sonnet she had written less than a week ago:

> How do I love thee? Let me count the ways.
> I love thee to the depth and breadth and height
> My soul can reach, when feeling out of sight
> For the ends of Being and ideal Grace.
> I love thee to the level of everyday's
> Most quiet need, by sun and candle-light.

I love thee freely, as men strive for Right;
I love thee purely, as they turn from Praise.
I love thee with the passion put to use
In my old griefs, and with my childhood's faith.
I love thee with a love I seemed to lose
With my lost saints,—I love thee with the breath,
Smiles, tears, of all my life!—and, if God choose,
I shall but love thee better after death.

There was her answer. And perfect love worked miracles.

She placed the sonnets in a stout envelope. They were her most perfect work. Someday, perhaps, in the years to come, she would have the courage to show them to the person to whom they had been written. But no other eye would ever see them.

For once she would have been quite as well pleased if either of her sisters had forgone the bedtime visit which they had fallen into the habit of making since Papa had ceased his. Then a sharp feeling of guilt and pain shot across her heart. Some night soon she might be beyond the sound of Henrietta's gay laughter and hungry for the understanding love in Arabel's blue eyes.

Tonight they both came, and behind them was Wilson, bearing large books of wallpaper samples, which Henrietta directed her to place on the nearest table while she and Arabel drew their chairs close beside Ba's sofa.

"We'll show you the papers we like for the drawing rooms, Ba," Henrietta began eagerly, "and the one I've chosen for my bedroom. Now love, look over these for this room. The pattern with the roses would be sweet, although Arabel inclines to this blue design."

Despite her efforts to make a show of concentration and eagerness, Ba saw little and cared less. It seemed an eternity before Arabel declared that Ba was too fatigued to be bothered any more.

As she passed Ba on her way out, she laid her cool cheek against her sister's hot one, murmuring, "I've sent Wilson after hot milk for you, Ba darling. And I won't be surprised if Mr. Browning knows the way to Reigate—or wherever we go."

She meant to be comforting, Ba knew, but every word anyone said on the subject set the pulse in Ba's throat throbbing.

When Wilson arrived with the milk, Ba's hands were too unsteady to hold the glass. She set it down hurriedly. "Wilson," she began, and then again, "Wilson—"

"Yes, Miss Ba?"

Ba swallowed twice before she could manage to say anything more than "Wilson—" stupidly for the third time. Then, at her final effort, she succeeded in stammering, "Tomorrow—we will be going, you and I, to St. Marylebone's Church. Ten-thirty will be a good time, I think."

"Yes, Miss Ba," said Wilson encouragingly and waited eagerly for the next disclosure. It was no overly strange event now for Miss Ba to make excursions from Wimpole Street, and surely nothing about a perfectly ordinary church just a few streets away should cause this nervous embarrassment—unless they were going for a particular purpose.

The color was alternately creeping up and dying out

of Ba's cheeks. She was intent on plaiting the folds of her nightrobe. "We—Mr. Browning will be there to meet us, with a friend of his—and Mr. Browning and I will be—married!" Her voice was almost inaudible. "Oh, Wilson, can I ask you to do me the favor of standing up with me? I cannot ask my sisters you know."

A combination of startled surprise and delight dawned on Wilson's usually impassive face. "Miss Ba, it will be the happiest deed of my life," she breathed. Her eyes shone with adoration. "Oh, Miss Ba, don't think I haven't seen it coming, but I thought you'd be asking Mrs. Jameson, or likely Mrs. Hedley. But to think you've asked me, Lily Wilson!" Then a sudden thought brought a trace of anxiety to the excited voice. "Will you be needing me afterward, Miss Ba? You're going to Italy?"

"Oh, Wilson! Yes!" Ba nodded in eager assurance. "We've talked about that, Mr. Browning and I. We'll be going to Italy as you guessed—not tomorrow, but very, very soon. And Mr. Browning said he would as soon sail in the hold of a merchant ship and dine on bread and water as to go without you. He said it was unthinkable. But if you should choose to go home to your own people—" Ba's breath caught at the unwelcome thought that this could be possible. "Of course, it is for you to decide. You must think, Wilson. You will be in a strange land, with a strange language, different customs—"

What happened next startled Ba and affected her so that she remembered it the rest of her life. She had known Wilson was loyal, loving, and faithful, but she had never seen her rather plain Scotch face swept with such a light of devotion, and she had certainly never expected to hear Wilson's ordinary monotone take on an almost musical sound and hear her quote: "whither thou goest, I will go, ... thy people shall be my people."

"Oh, Wilson," gulped Ba. "Oh, Wilson—" And then she suddenly crumpled, and the awful tension of the past two days went out in low wrenching sobs, and Wilson gathered her into her arms, and comforted her, and both of them forgot they were mistress and maid.

"My sisters," Ba wept. "If only I could tell my precious sisters!"

"Aye, aye, I ken! I ken!" murmured Wilson, lapsing into her native tongue as she often did when she was stirred. "But they'll be glad for you, Miss Ba! They'll rejoice to have you well-loved and happy and hearty, and you'll be all that with Mr. Browning, I'll warrant you, miss, for he's the finest gentleman ever walked in England."

She soothed her mistress gently until the sobs lessened and the tense figure relaxed, and then all at once she was briskness again. "Mercy on us, look at the time! Near to one of the morning! We must get you to bed, Miss Ba. You'll need a sound sleep against the day."

However much Ba needed it, she had no sleep that night. She lay awake, with a myriad thoughts beating on her brain—thoughts of her father, as she had known him in childhood—generous, ready to please her, proud of her childish poems; of her gentle, retiring mother, who had died just when Ba needed her most; of her proud, vinegarish grandmother who had professed to be displeased with her namesake's poetry, but who left her a substantial legacy; of her Uncle Samuel, who used to claim he loved her better than her father did, and had left her a legacy, too. She thought of Torquay and Bro—even now it was torture to remember; and of Arabel and Henrietta— would they be blamed when she was gone? And her brothers, they would understand, surely! But dearest Papa —would he ever forgive?

On and on through the night her thoughts raced and tumbled until the dawn. She still lay rigid when Wilson brought her breakfast tray.

Ba never knew whether she ate or not, but Wilson told her afterward that she seemed able to swallow only the coffee.

"Now don't fret, miss. I've seen to everything. I've been telling Miss Arabel you are driving to Mr. Boyd's this morning, and that'll be no lie. You will do so after your ceremony, so that will explain the morning excursion."

Ba sat dumbly at her dressing table and let Wilson do whatever she would. The face that stared at her from the glass was pinched and terrified and white. What a bride for Robert—Robert, who deserved the best! She prayed passionately for strength and that the feeling of illness and dizziness which was coming in waves might be abated. Wilson was bringing out her best gown of silver-gray silk with deep lace at neck and wrists and her fashionable dove-colored bonnet. She would have protested that these garments were too conspicuous for a simple morning call, but instinct warned her not to waste her strength on such a trivial matter.

When Wilson said gently, "Ready, miss? We'd best be going," she stood up docilely enough, though she was shaking so violently that Wilson had a sinking sensation as she wondered how she was to get Miss Ba downstairs.

Somehow the descent was accomplished; somehow Ba walked out of the house; but by a mischance the cab Wilson had ordered was not at the door. Nor did it arrive. Ten precious minutes passed. Ba had grown fearfully white and Wilson was seized with desperation.

"We'd best walk to the hackstand on the corner, miss, and pick up a cab there." She passed her arm steadily around her mistress. "It's not a far cry."

"Yes," said Ba bravely. "We must not be late."

But the sun was hot, the London air really oppressive; Ba had spent a sleepless night and had eaten nothing. Before they reached the stand she was staggering so dangerously that Wilson was in a panic. Her anxious eye caught sight of a chemist's shop, and she piloted Ba to the door.

"Bring me some sal volatile. Be quick! My lady faints!" she cried to the startled clerk.

Ba was praying, I said I wouldn't fail. Grant me strength. Grant me strength to keep my promise.

Perhaps both prayer and smelling salts helped, for gradually a faint color touched Ba's cheeks. At the sight Wilson gave a great sigh of relief, said a fervent prayer of her own, and sped away to summon a cab.

St. Marylebone Church was nearly a hundred years old, a rather uninviting and grimy structure with heavy doors, but Ba wouldn't have known whether she stood in St.

Paul's or Arabel's favorite chapel. All she was aware of was that Robert and another figure were waiting at the door, and once her hands were in Robert's the world righted itself and new strength flooded her body.

"My cousin, Jim Silverthorne, Ba," Robert introduced them. "Jim, Miss Barrett." Ba raised her eyes to the very young, very curious cousin who was to be Robert's best man, gave him her hand and whispered, "So kind of you to come."

"Delighted to be here." Jim Silverthorne's large paw closed over Ba's small fingers. Privately he was thinking that his cousin Robert had made a queer choice of sweethearts, but that was Robert's concern, not his.

"The minister is waiting," Robert told Ba, and drew her arm gently through his. There was no trembling on Ba's part now. She went slowly but firmly up the aisle to the altar.

The combination of two famous poets and a special license made the minister almost as nervous as the bridal couple. Robert gave his responses with sure conviction and, steadied by his handclasp and the beautiful words of the marriage service, Ba went through the brief ceremony without faltering.

So between eleven-fifteen and eleven-thirty on the morning of September 12, 1846, Elizabeth Barrett Barrett and Robert Browning were married, with Lily Wilson, lady's maid, and Jim Silverthorne, who spent his days in the hunting field, as witnesses.

Afterward the Brownings had exactly three minutes together while Wilson called another cab.

"I will not call again, dearest, since I cannot ask for
'Mrs. Browning,' and I will not ask for 'Miss Barrett.' " He
helped her into the cab. "But you will come to me—and
soon."

"Yes!" Her eyes were on her wedding ring.

"My dearest Ba! Be good to her, Wilson, and stay by
her."

Then he gave the order to drive to St. John's Wood and
was gone.

By what must have been some special act of a merciful
Providence, Mr. Boyd's doctor was visiting him when
Mrs. Browning and Wilson arrived. Wilson seized the
opportunity to say to the maid, "Miss Ba is still nervous
and upset over wee Flush's being stolen, you know, and
not a wink of sleep did she have last night, miss. Could
she lie down a few minutes while the doctor is with
Mr. Boyd?"

Of course Miss Barrett could lie down! The maid led
the way into the rather dingy sitting room, apologizing
for the shabby couch. It looked like heaven itself to Ba,
and she gratefully let Wilson tuck her up on it.

"Now I will go back to Wimpole Street and fetch Miss
Arabel and Miss Henrietta," Wilson said cheerfully. She
bent to adjust a pillow, and observed in a low tone, "It
would be well to remove the ring."

Merciful Heaven! Ba gasped in alarm at forgetting the
telltale article!

The half-hour rest revived her a little, and then she was
taken upstairs and made to share Mr. Boyd's lunch, and
to talk and talk, until at weary last, her sisters appeared.

Then she rose and kissed the old man for the last time in their lives.

Out in the carriage Henrietta gave the driver a command to drive to Hampstead, and Ba didn't dare offer a protest. "It's a glorious day." Henrietta looked her sister full in the face. "And the drive will do you good. You're looking awfully pale, love, almost ill."

"It's the heat. I can't say you're looking too spritely yourselves," Ba murmured, trying to turn the tables skillfully, "especially Arabel. Such a grave face, darling."

"Well, we were so disturbed about you, Ba, when we found you and Wilson missing," Henrietta confessed soberly, leaning over to kiss her sister. "Arabel forgot what Wilson had said about the cab for this morning and we had all sorts of fancies about things happening to you."

"Oh, what nonsense!" Ba tried to speak boldly. "What did you think was happening to me, pray?"

Arabel lifted her serious blue eyes and gave her sister a searchingly grave look.

"I thought you were being married," she said.

SUNDAY was a nightmare to Ba Browning. Friends of the Barretts had arrived from Hertfordshire, and everybody—Arabel, Henrietta, George, Henry, Alfred, Stormie, Sette and Occy, together with Papa and the guests, assembled in Ba's room after dinner. Ba, beginning to have the horrible obsession that every time she opened her mouth she would betray the secret of yesterday's wedding, felt as though a dozen swords were pointed at her from every direction. Luckily she wasn't naturally talkative, and there were plenty of people present who were used to covering Ba's silences, so no one noticed that she sat even more mute than usual.

In a momentary silence the peal of church bells rang out on the soft afternoon air, and one of the visitors inquired idly, "What bells are those?"

"Marylebone Church bells," answered Henrietta, who happened to be standing behind Ba's chair, and Ba nearly leaped from her seat. She cast a nervous glance around her to see if anyone had noticed, but the din of conversation began again, and if there had been any danger, it was past. Ba sighed. Her head was aching so violently she felt as if it would split into two halves, one for each shoulder, but she didn't dare complain about it for fear of arousing Arabel's already alert suspicions.

If only they would go—all of them, so that she could snatch a few minutes to write a note to Robert. There were so many things she must say—so much they must decide. Finally, after much lingering and several false starts, everyone had departed, and the room was filled with a blessed emptiness. Ba took a deep breath of relief and crossed the room to find her writing desk. She had hardly begun her letter to her husband when there was a gentle tap on her door, the knob turned, and Mr. Kenyon appeared.

"Have you a welcome for me after all your other guests, my dear?"

Ba jumped and shut the desk with an undeniably guilty blush.

"Why—oh—of course!" she stammered with a wide departure from the truth. The rotund little man came in, sat down opposite her, looking at her through his thick spectacles, and his eyes suddenly seemed to Ba to reach the rim of his glasses all around.

"When did you see Browning?" he demanded. Now why had he opened his conversation with *that* question?

Ba knew she was blushing, but she made a neat evasion. "He was here on Friday. Did you ever know such warmth in September? Do you advise us to go to Reigate or Tunbridge?"

"Either will be beneficial," said Mr. Kenyon patiently. "When do you see Browning again?"

Dearest, he saw something, but not all, she scribbled in her letter when she could go on with it. *I feel so bewildered. I feel so as if I had slipped down over the wall into somebody's garden.* She asked him to beseech his father's and mother's forgiveness, and to ask his sister to love her. But she continued on a triumphal note. *I have a right now openly to love you!*

That was the beginning of the longest and most difficult week the Brownings would ever know. Since Robert could not bring himself to appear at Wimpole Street and ask for the honor of seeing "Miss Barrett," the only link between them was the post. (It never seems to have occurred to either one of them that it was downright funny for Robert to be able to address envelopes to his wife as "Miss Barrett" when he considered it would be a fib to ask for her at her door.) They kept the postmen of London and New Cross busy. Eighteen letters went back and forth while they tried desperately to make the right plans.

It was a week of great strain for Ba and Robert. Ba quailed at the thought that something, anything, might betray her. "And I shall be killed!" she wailed to Robert. He had his horrible misgivings that she might be spirited away to some inaccessible spot before she could notify him, or that her strength would crumble under the strain.

By this time both the Brownings were acutely conscious that neither of them was more than half-alive without the other.

Finally they agreed to leave London on Saturday, the 19th of September, whereupon Robert Browning promptly lost his head and behaved like the proverbial bridegroom, getting his dates and schedules for trains and boats completely muddled. The utterly rattled man wrote:

You propose Saturday . . . *Nothing leaves Southampton according to* to-day's *advertisement till* Tuesday . . . *the days seemed changed to* Tuesdays *and* Fridays . . . *Provoking! I will go to town directly to the railway office and enquire particularly—getting the time-table also. Under these circumstances, we have only the choice of Dieppe . . . or the Sunday morning Havre-packet, at 9 A.M.*

But at five o'clock that same afternoon (and it was now Thursday) he was writing again. He'd made a mistake! He had looked at the sailings from Le Havre instead of Southampton! She must be at Vauxhall station by four o'clock.

By this time Mr. Browning didn't know whether he was reading a time-table or a seed catalogue. He sent another note Thursday evening in which he confessed he had confused the South of England Steam Company with the South Western. "There must be then two companies," complained the muddled man.

In the end it was sheltered Ba who caught the mistakes and explained them to Robert, the experienced traveler. The packet would leave the Royal Pier, Southampton, at

nine. The train left Vauxhall Station at five, to arrive at
eight. She would leave Wimpole Street between half past
three and four o'clock and drive to Hodgson's, the sta-
tioner's, and he could meet her there.

"My own best Ba," exclaimed Robert in the last letter
he ever wrote to her, "how thankful I am you have seen
my blunder!"

Meanwhile, Mrs. Browning had been going through her
own chaos of confusion and torment. There was the matter of hers and Wilson's luggage. Robert had warned her
not to bring much, since every ounce counted, and Wilson had skillfully reduced their wardrobes to one box and
one carpetbag. But how to get them out of the house un-
seen? Every day the tension of the situation and the
separation from Robert frayed Ba's nerves until she was
afraid that when she actually did reach the shelter of the
Southampton packet she would snap altogether.

There came another sleepless Friday night. But this one
she spent in writing letters. First she wrote separately to
each of her sisters and brothers; and then she forced herself to begin the letter to Papa. *Papa, I am married. . . .
I hope you will not be too displeased—*

Earlier she had written a final letter to her husband.

*By to-morrow at this time, I shall have you only, to love
me—my beloved!*

*You only! As if one said God only. And we shall have
Him beside, I pray of Him.*

*I shall send to your address at New Cross your Hanmer's
poems—and the two dear books you gave me, which I do
not like to leave here and am afraid of hurting by taking*

*them with me. Will you ask our Sister to put the parcel
into a drawer, so as to keep it for us?*

*Your letters to me I take with me, let the "ounces" cry
out aloud, ever so. I tried to leave them, and I could not.
That is, they would not be left: it was not my fault—I will
not be scolded. . . .*

*Remind your mother and father of me affectionately
and gratefully—and your Sister too! Would she think it
too bold of me to say our Sister, if she heard it on the last
page?*

*Do you pray for me to-night, Robert? Pray for me, and
love me, that I may have courage, feeling both—*

Your own BA

Both Ba and Wilson moved in a daze the next day.
Robert's prayers seemed speedily granted, for Ba had none
of the sick sensations she had battled the Saturday before.
Now it was as if she had no feeling whatever. Most of the
family had gone to Little Bookham, where George had
finally selected a house, and would not return until din-
nertime. Ba had sent word she would like to see Arabel,
but Arabel had gone to some chapel affair. Well, it would
have been hard to say this particular farewell to Arabel.

Even Flush was uncannily quiet as Wilson carried him
downstairs. And then they had shut the door of 50 Wimpole Street behind them. Was it forever?

Ba's mind was always a blank about that special cab
ride through the streets of London. Her first clear recol-
lection after she stepped into the vehicle was Wilson's low
exclamation, "Aye, Mr. Browning's here. Look out,
ma'am, and see!"

Robert Browning was indeed there, pacing up and down before the door of Hodgson's. At the rumbling of the cab he halted, looked up, flung up an arm in greeting and grinned beatifically. He looked like a different person. Never again would he have to exert caution or concealment about his love for Ba. He could proclaim it to the world now, and he stood fine and strong and jubilant.

"You're in splendid time, Ba!" he cried joyously as he flung open the door and leaped in beside her. "To the Vauxhall Station, driver!"

Ba had been afraid that she would be timid, even with Robert, on the train journey. She had seen a railway train only once before, on a drive with Mr. Kenyon, and the engine had seemed to leap at her like a great black mole. But when Robert lifted her into the coach—which looked like an overgrown stagecoach—and the wheels really began to move, after her first few minutes of panic, she found herself smiling. It was an odd sensation, this traveling swiftly and sometimes a little jerkily, but, cradled in Robert's arm, it wasn't uncomfortable at all. As a matter of fact, Ba liked it.

She smiled into Robert's anxious face. "The boxes are safely sent. And Wilson has been perfect to me. I begin to think that none are so bold as the timid when they are fairly roused."

"Miss Ba—begging your pardon—Mrs. Browning has been perfect herself, if I may take the liberty of saying so, sir," said Wilson, trying to look as settled and composed as her mistress.

"Both of you have been wonderful beyond belief," said Robert fervently.

He had been anxious about the train trip, fearful that the motion and excitement might make Ba ill, as it did some people, but Ba was eager and curious and excited about everything. At the end of the trip she seemed brighter and rosier than she had been in weeks. So far— good!

Now the voyage across the channel lay before them. It promised to be a pleasant night, with just enough of a breeze to send the fast packet cutting through the water at a nice clip. Could Ba be expected to escape being sick? For a minute Robert looked grim, and Wilson clicked her tongue against her teeth apprehensively. She knew what he was thinking—she had been worrying about the same thing for the past hour herself.

Skillfully Robert Browning piloted the two women and Flush aboard the packet and settled them in chairs before he returned to the pier to see about their luggage. He marveled at the way Ba had braved her first railway ride and stepped up the gangplank of the packet. Was it child-like trust or her perfect love which had cast out fear? A mixture of both, perhaps, but even Robert had yet to learn that, small and frail though she was, Ba possessed an unquenchable spirit which always enabled her to meet an occasion.

They sailed at nine, just as twilight was settling over the English coast, turning the water to mother-of-pearl and pricking the sky with the first stars. Ba was weary, but she lay wrapped in enchantment, her hand in Robert's.

The sight of the shore lights gradually receding, the sound of the lapping waves against the boat, the brightening stars in the vast arch above her, were all foreign to Ba. She found them strange but somehow good and oddly stirring. She even liked the sound of the sailor's voices and their quick-moving feet about the deck. Somehow she wasn't moved to talk, but she smiled confidently into her husband's eyes when he bent anxiously over her.

It was apparent, however, that Wilson couldn't share her mistress' delight in this new adventure. Wilson was miserable almost before they were out of sight of land, and within half an hour Robert and a steward had half carried her below.

"Poor Wilson," mourned Ba with genuine tenderness. "Should I go to her, Robert?"

"No, no." Mr. Browning put a restraining arm around her. "It's best to leave her quite alone. I know! You are comfortable?"

The moon had risen now, transforming everything on the deck and making a path of glory across the channel. It had been so long since Ba had seen moonlight that its magic seemed incredible.

"Comfortable, Ba?" Robert was repeating. She turned to him then, and spoke with sincere simplicity, "I was just thinking, Robert, 'my cup runneth over!'"

A DAY and a half later the trio arrived in Paris. Each had been haunted by unspoken qualms that the journey, coming as the climax to the strain of the past week, might be the final straw for Ba.

But Ba amazed herself and delighted her husband. She sat through her new experiences with wide-eyed wonder and eagerness. She liked the railway. The channel crossing she thought was beautiful, lying contentedly in her chair until the sea air and the night sounds had lulled her to sleep. In the carriage from Le Havre to Paris she had so much to see that she had no time to be ill.

"How the sunshine glistens!" she exclaimed. "And the blueness of the sky—is it always so? And the air is so—so brilliant—and yet not sharp. It makes one feel free to breathe!"

Robert laughed joyously. "If just these few miles from the ugly old London damp make you feel free, what will the miracle be when we're settled at Pisa? This is God's gift of pure air, my own Ba, instead of London's soot and fog which offended your lungs for so long."

Wilson, huddled in a far corner of the carriage, moaned faintly. Exhausted by her violent seasickness, and dizzy and miserable from the jouncing of the carriage, she would have given all she possessed to be back in soot- and fog-laden London.

Flush wasn't taking kindly to the expedition either. He lay shivering in the folds of Ba's gown, too bewildered even to whimper. No salted cream cheese or macaroons! No cream and coffee in a purple drinking cup! Flush did not approve of the junketings which had plagued him lately.

In Paris, however, the excitement and tension of the past month caught up with Ba. She had a day's illness which scared Robert out of his wits, especially since Wilson had taken to her bed also. In a fit of desperation he dispatched a note to Mrs. Jameson at the address she had given Ba, and to his great relief, that lady came to the rescue. With her pale eyes, no eyebrows, colorless lips, and red hair, she couldn't have been styled a beauty, but it is safe to say that the Brownings had never seen a more radiant woman. Luckily Mrs. Jameson was the sort of person who could bring comfort out of chaos in a miraculously short time.

She listened with sympathy as Robert poured out his story.

"Quite right, Browning. Perfectly done. Yes, it was the

only thing done in the only way. Now take me—" her eyes twinkled at him, "take me to your wife."

Looking at Ba lying there limply on the hotel bed, Mrs. Jameson had a flood of misgivings. The little bride did look horribly ill. Then the good Samaritan broke into smiles, bent over, and kissed her.

"My love, what a surprise! I despaired of you when I left England. I considered you chained to 50 Wimpole Street for the rest of your life. I see now what you meant when you said you were going to Italy with 'efficient companionship.' And I was right about the elopement. You wonderful people, both of you. And Browning tells me you have made excellent plans. I also hear Wilson is ill. I must see to her comfort too. Browning, fetch me hot water and a towel, and Ba's brush and comb. This will freshen you so much, my dear." She worked gently with the articles when the perturbed Robert brought them. "Have either of you dined yet?"

Ba shook her head wearily and Robert confessed neither of them had had any appetite that day.

Mrs. Jameson shook her head with emphatic disapproval. "Quite wrong. Altogether. Browning, you find the concierge and have him fetch soup, the white of a chicken, rolls, and coffee. That's for Ba and Wilson. You suit yourself. Only eat!"

Ba's eyes followed Robert until he was safely gone. Then she whispered, "I—I knew it would be wrong—to do this. See how I am sick at the very beginning, and a burden—"

"Nonsense!" Mrs. Jameson interrupted vigorously.

"You're not sick—just fatigued and excited and nervous.
Of course you did right! You're children of light, both of
you."

When Browning returned with the food, she admon-
ished, "Now, mind, Ba, eat, and while you do I'll look in
on Wilson."

She departed and Robert took the chair she had vacated,
coaxing Ba to swallow the first food she had managed that
day. She found the savory broth was tempting and the
morsels of chicken and bits of rolls were not as impossible
as they had been before. By the time she had drunk the
coffee, she was a different Ba.

When Mrs. Jameson returned, she eyed Ba with approval. "Now, listen to what I am proposing. The apartment above me in my hotel is vacant. Take it, Browning,
and stay in Paris for a week. By then Ba will be rested and
Wilson well, and you can proceed to Pisa at your ease."

The Brownings looked at each other and then at their
benefactress with dawning delight. Despite her odd looks
and commanding ways, Mrs. Jameson, next to Robert
Browning himself, was the best person in the world for
Ba. Brisk, but not rudely curt, affectionate without being
fulsome, she inspired Ba with confidence, yet did not
weary her by urging her to attempt the impossible. Also,
she was a fine match for Robert's enthusiasms and boundless energy, and by late afternoon the Browning party was
installed in the apartment in the Hôtel de la Ville de Paris,
a much more sunny and airy place than Robert had hastily
engaged earlier in the day. Flush, apparently convinced
by now that neither he nor his mistress was in the hands

of bandits, was in full spirits, and even Wilson took a less jaundiced view of the world.

Ba had no chance to get acquainted with Paris that first week of her honeymoon. Robert did venture to take her to the Louvre one day, but for the most part she rested against the remainder of their journey to Italy, while Mrs. Jameson and Robert mapped out plans for the easiest and most pleasant route. Before the week was up, Mrs. Jameson had another proposition for the Brownings. Suppose she and her seventeen-year-old niece, Gerardine Bate, who was accompanying her, traveled to Pisa with the bride and groom? She had brought Gerardine abroad to give her an artistic education, and where could she find a better place for that than Italy?

Not a particularly private wedding trip, but everyone concerned snatched at the idea with delight. Both Robert and Ba loved Mrs. Jameson and enjoyed her sparkling companionship. Wilson was pleased and relieved, for much as she admired and trusted Mr. Browning, she secretly thought he had a tendency to go to pieces in a crisis, which Mrs. Jameson certainly did not. As for Geddie Bate, the romantic prospect of spending two or three weeks in the company of two famous and handsome poets (not that she had read a single line either of them had written) who had just eloped under the most fascinating circumstances, made her hug herself with glee.

The party traveled southward across France by easy stages. They paused for two days at Vaucluse where six hundred years before the Italian poet-monk Petrarch had written his love poems in praise of Laura, the woman he immortalized. There Robert was seized by a sudden impulse and laughingly snatched Ba up and waded out into the shallow water until he could seat her on a thronelike rock, an experience which made her gasp and laugh, frightened and elated at the same time. Standing on the shore the frantic Flush saw his mistress in what seemed to him dire peril, and he promptly swam out to her, whereupon Robert baptized him in the name of Petrarch.

Somewhere along the road Mrs. Jameson and Geddie presented Ba with a pomegranate, because, long before she ever heard from him, Ba had one of the characters in a poem of hers read to his sweetheart, Lady Geraldine:

. . . from Browning some "Pomegranate," which, if cut deep down the middle,
Shows a heart within blood-tinctured, of a veined humanity.

Ba was thrilled as she borrowed a knife and proceeded to cut her pomegranate "deep down the middle." Eating it was a different matter. Even Wilson laughed as Ba grimaced and confessed that it caused her much confusion of face, and that hereafter she would admire pomegranates and olives on a shelf.

At Orléans the first letters from England arrived. Ba waited tensely while Robert went to the post office, and she knew instantly by the look on her husband's face when he returned that he brought letters from her family. She could only hold out her hands, growing paler and paler as she saw the familiar seals and handwriting. There was Papa's black seal, the griffin; Henrietta's dashing scrawl, Occy's, George's, Henry's—all her family's missives. And what did they hold?

Finally she lifted pleading eyes to her husband who was watching her with tender anxiety, heedless of his own letters.

"Please, Robert, will you leave me alone for—for a while?"

"At least let me sit near you?" he asked gently. But she shook her head in such desperation that he rose reluctantly, kissed her, and went out of the room, closing the door quietly.

George's letter. She would read that first, for George, solemn and ponderous as he always was, had always been her loyal advocate. Next to her sisters, she thought George was the one member of her family who had a real affection for her. And then she caught her breath and surprised pain gathered in her face. George's letter was harsh, lashing out at her in almost vindictive language. Carefully she replaced it in its envelope and took up Alfred's. His was the same. Accusing her of doing a sinful thing and deliberately turning against her family. She could wait no longer. Swiftly she slit the envelope sealed with the black griffin. Her father's letter was what she'd expected, but it made bitter reading. He was merciless, unreasoning in his anger. He told her he considered that he no longer had a daughter named Elizabeth. To him she was as dead as her brothers Edward and Samuel. He would never see, write to her, or speak of her again.

Ba said a quick prayer for strength and went through the rest of her mail. Her brothers' letters were all the same. Echoes of Papa's. They thought of her as a traitor and a disgrace. She had no love for any of them, they said.

Arabel's and Henrietta's messages she purposely saved
for the last, and when Robert returned, he found her just
able to cry from the balm of their words. She thrust all the
letters into his hands with the one grief-stricken cry.

"To Papa's I have to bow my head. He is my parent and
does what he believes is right. But it is hard to have dear
George write to me with the point of a sword."

Reading the letters through, her husband grew more
and more grim. At the end he begged Ba to let his own
love erase all the bitterness. " 'They know not what they
do,' " he quoted earnestly. "But my Ba will have faith and
love and believe that what has been said was done out of
haste and sorrow at losing you, and did not come from
their hearts."

Ba could only cling to him, shaken and miserable.

"You do think Papa will forgive us in time? Surely he
will melt?"

Robert Browning would not promise what he didn't believe. He had never seen or heard any indication that Mr.
Barrett was capable of melting. As indeed he wasn't. John
Kenyon braved him on several occasions, trying to bring
him to his senses. Robert Browning, he assured his cousin,
was a man any father would gladly see his daughter
marry. And Mr. Barrett favored him with a stony look and
replied with acid in his voice.

"No doubt! Whatever I have heard of Mr. Browning
has been to his credit. I have no objection to him as a man
—but my daughter should have been thinking of entering
another world instead of marriage!"

Then, perhaps for the first time in his life, tactful Mr.

Kenyon lost his temper. "So she should!" he snapped. "So she should indeed! A world of freedom and beauty, where she'll be loved and appreciated as a human being. And thank God, she's entered it!"

But that day at Orléans had brought mail for Robert too. His letters were shining silver against Ba's black clouds. His father wrote, "Kiss your wife for me." His mother sent her love. Sarianna Browning said she was sending a writing desk to her "sister."

Mr. Kenyon had written a letter to them both, praising them for what they had done. He considered, he said, that Ba had risked her life and that she'd done right to risk it. He had enjoyed their separate company and loved them as separate individuals, now he looked forward to enjoying and loving them together.

Many of Robert's friends had sent cordial congratulations, but the letter which pleased both of them most came from cynical Thomas Carlyle. *Certainly,* he wrote in his ponderous style, *if ever there was a union indicated by the finger of Heaven itself ... it seems to me, from all I could see and know of it, to be this!*

In the presence of this warm, spontaneous approval and affection, Ba knew she would be wrong to let her family's bitterness bedevil hers and Robert's lives, and she made an heroic effort to put it aside. It was a grief, but it couldn't and didn't outweigh the happiness which surged higher every day.

By the first week of October Robert proudly brought Ba into the city of their dreams. They took rooms in the Collegio Ferdinando, and there Mrs. Jameson and Geddie

prepared to leave them. Greatly to Mrs. Jameson's amazement, Ba was thrilled with traveling, and prospered every
day of their journey, whether it was by boat, carriage, or
railway.

"My dear, how do you do it?" Mrs. Jameson shook her
head unbelievingly over the miracle. "I confess a day on
the railway exhausts me to the point of illness. Yet you are
fresher than a rose."

Ba's smile was roguish. "Do you have Robert to cushion
and comfort and entertain you? But you see, dear Mona
Nina, that I grew so weary with lying still back in
Wimpole Street, that all this traveling is rest to me. Do
you call me really improved?"

All day Mrs. Jameson had been remembering the Ba she
had first known in Wimpole Street, a fragile little invalid
with pain-haunted eyes and a pinched face shadowed by
lusterless curls. Then she remembered the Ba of one short
year ago, for whom it was a real achievement to be carried
downstairs to a carriage, and who was making her first
feeble attempts to walk after nearly five years of being
bedridden.

And now—could this be Ba, standing upright on her
feet in an airy, sunlit room of the Collegio Ferdinando,
free, eager, her eyes bright with hope, her cheeks beginning to be round and touched with pink?

For a minute Mrs. Jameson dared not trust her voice.
This must have been the way the people felt in Biblical
days when they witnessed a miracle, for what she was be-
holding was a miracle wrought by Robert Browning's

gentle persistence, stimulating personality, and over-whelming love.

"Oh, dear Mona Nina," Ba was saying, "don't you think I look even a little better?"

Robert had come to stand behind his wife, clasping his hands about her waist. "She isn't quite the forlorn bride you found in Paris, would you say?" he asked quizzically. "Of course I grant you I am prejudiced."

Mrs. Jameson found her voice then and shook her head decisively. "No, my dear. No, I can't call you improved. You are transformed!"

Ba laughed. "Why, the constant change of air and the continued fine weather make me better and better. I like the new sights and the movement!" She suddenly had the elfin expression Mr. Kenyon had noticed so often. "My spirits rise. I live—I can adapt myself. Do you understand, Robert? I think I belong here."

Ba had achieved paradise. She was in Pisa.

OVER and over again during her first months in Pisa, Ba had to pinch herself to be convinced that she was still very much in the flesh and inhabiting an earthly world.

A ten-day deluge had been the Brownings' welcome to Pisa, but after that the weather repented and offered weeks of perpetual balminess, with such exquisitely blue and cloudless skies and soft winds fragrant with the scent of oranges, that Ba declared the calendar certainly must be a hoax. She refused to believe the month was truly November; it had to be April!

Everything she saw and did seemed incredible. Was it really Ba Barrett Browning who went for daily walks with her husband, and when she was tired, dropped down upon an ancient stone wall to admire the lizards? Was it possible that, when the year was at November, one was obliged to seek the shady side of the streets to avoid the excessive heat, and that one could behold the startling sight of women wearing furs and carrying parasols?

And to think of the immense oranges still wearing their green leaves the *padrone* of the house brought to her!

The news from home made them both doubly thankful that they had escaped London when they did. England was paying for her balmy winter of last year and was in the grip of exceptionally early snows and extreme cold. Ba shivered just to read of it.

"I would be frozen along with the water pipes!" she exclaimed, looking up from Arabel's letter. "And the smoke from the faulty fireplaces in Little Bookham would have been the end of me."

"My sister says the same." Robert nodded. "I am altogether glad we came just when we did, Ba. Bringing a soot-covered snow-maiden with me to Italy would have been somewhat inconvenient!" He loved the chuckle Ba had acquired these last weeks. "And if your sisters could see you as you are now, dearest, they could never grieve for your empty place."

Ba knew it couldn't be his loving flattery. Only that morning Wilson had exclaimed, "Oh, if Miss Henrietta and Miss Arabel could see you, ma'am—looking so rosy and plump and eating all your egg of a morning."

When the pretty, shy, rosy-faced little Italian maid appeared with hot roasted chestnuts, Ba nibbled them with a delight which was a far cry from the Wimpole Street days when eating was a labor and a punishment. Catching the pleased expression in Robert's eyes, she colored and laughed a little as she bent to give the demanding Flush a chestnut. "Do I look so greedy that you gaze at me so, Robert?"

The Browning laughter came easily nowadays. "I was looking at a miracle," he told her joyously. "To behold you eating voluntarily—that is a miracle of Italy, surely!"

Everything about Italy had been a miracle. "It is my own especial fairy tale, this Italy," said Ba softly.

Flush approved of Italy, too. Like his Miss Barrett, he had freedom here. He could roam the streets (and pick up fleas) without fear of dog-stealers. He admired roast chestnuts, and apparently soon spoke a fluent Italian to little Italian dogs. Above all, he became strongly attached to Browning. Evidently he was quick to grasp the fact that a dog may bite a fiancé, and be forgiven, but when the fiancé turns into a husband, it is high time to change policies.

As the autumn and winter passed, the Browning household, with the exception of Wilson, reveled in Italy. Poor Wilson was having a difficult time acclimating herself. Ba had a natural talent for picking up languages, but Wilson was slow about it. Perhaps she was homesick, and the nostalgia reached a stage where she became physically ill. Finally she confessed to Ba that she had a good deal of pain in her left side and had spent eight shillings for pills, which didn't seem strong enough. She asked Mr. Browning to buy her something stronger.

Mr. Browning exclaimed that eight shillings' worth of pills was enough to kill anyone. He wouldn't take the responsibility of getting more, but he would take her to the doctor; whereupon Wilson became instantly better. But one night when Ba was bathing her feet in hot water, Wilson dropped down on the sofa in a shivering fit, moaning that she was very ill.

Ba fled down the corridor and dispatched Robert for the doctor. It was a stormy night and late.

"Suppose he won't come?" Robert suggested as he struggled into his coat.

"Oh, he must!" Ba spoke in agitation. "Or I shall go fetch him myself."

Remembering the episode of the dog thieves, Browning decided it would be best to persuade Dr. Cook himself. Both of them returned shortly. Dr. Cook found nothing seriously wrong with Wilson. The change of food and climate probably had caused the mischief, climaxed with the poisonous quantity of pills, but a few days in bed would settle everything.

"But how will you get on, ma'am?" moaned Wilson. "This is all upside down. It's you as should be abed, and my place to be taking care of you."

Ba struggled against laughter, but she understood the loyalty under the left-handed remark and bent to kiss the flushed and anxious face.

"It's my day to repay some of the excellent and loving care you've given me," she assured Wilson. "I owe you the more because"—her voice filled with remorse—"it has been staying in Italy that has made you ill while I've been getting well and strong."

"But—but you're so little and helpless-like—" And the

woebegone tears of the normally energetic and efficient person who is suddenly laid low slid down Wilson's cheeks.

What no one, even those closest to her, ever seemed to realize was that fragile and dependent though Ba ordinarily was, when a challenging situation arose, she could contend with it with all the ardor of her headlong spirit.

Probably Robert was surprised (and if the truth must be told, so was she) to discover Ba's capabilities. She wrote home that *it is possible (in certain conditions of the human frame) to comb out and twist up one's own hair, and lace up one's very own stays, and cause hooks and eyes to meet behind one's very own back.*

Meals were no problem—they were sent in from a nearby restaurant. A maid and a manservant cared for the house, but Ba decided to prepare the invalid's toast and tea herself, with Robert fetching the kettle of water and intimating that it wasn't considered necessary to set fire to the bread in order to toast it.

But he carried the finished productions to Wilson's bedside with a flourish and observed with inordinate pride, "This is your tea, Wilson—just as Dr. Cook prescribes, and the handiwork of your mistress." Wilson regarded the tray with a doubtful eye; a fact which Ba, standing on the other side of the bed, was quick to appreciate.

"It's all perfectly safe, Wilson, I assure you. Mr. Browning poured the water over the tea and counseled me about the toast. Robert, you frighten poor Wilson! She probably is sure I don't know which end of a toasting fork to hold before the fire."

Despite her doubts as to toast and tea prepared by the Brownings, Wilson recovered rapidly. She had a fright when Ba told her she had consulted Dr. Cook about sending her home to England; the very thought of being parted from her beloved mistress and her adored Mr. Browning cured her of her homesickness. Thereafter Wilson would think of Italy as "home."

Early that winter Robert and Ba began to realize that it would be a good idea to provide more of their poems for the English and American public. Robert's books weren't exactly best sellers, but Ba's certainly were, and her publisher, Moxon, was clamoring for a new one. At the same time he said, a little tepidly, that he would consider a new edition of Robert's poems.

Ba could write anywhere. Usually she curled up in a big green velvet chair, her writing desk on her knees. If anyone interrupted her she would smile and tuck the tiny sheets away until her next free moment. Robert happened to be a person whose thoughts were only too easily jarred, and any disturbance could have distressing consequences for Robert and the poem he was struggling with. He fitted up a long narrow room in the apartment where he could retreat to toil and suffer in silence and privacy.

The long discipline of illness had taught Ba how to write whenever she needed to, regardless of pain or sleepless nights or other temptations. Robert Browning was an incurable paper-spoiler and had to wait desperately for the inspiration to write. If the inspiration dallied too long and didn't knock at his brain until nine o'clock at night, he stored it until the next day.

One day he stood at the window trying to capture a wayward rhyme and envying Ba her facile gift of words. Suddenly he was conscious of Ba standing behind him. She was stuffing something into his pocket.

"Do you know—" She gulped, and then plunged on breathlessly. "Do you know I once wrote some poems to you? There they are. You can tear them up afterward!"

Then she fled.

And so, finally, Ba's forty-four sonnets lay before her husband's eyes. He read first one and then another, on and on, hardly pausing. Never had he read anything like them —he, who thought he knew and understood and appreciated the fine music of his wife's poetry. These were different; these had been written with a pen dipped in splendid love, and the words sang with a glory which left him breathless. She had written lovely poems before, but these had greatness. To Robert they seemed the greatest sonnets since Shakespeare's. They left him awed and wondering.

When he came to the last one, with its triumphal climax,

How do I love thee? Let me count the ways

he stood up reverently and read it through again, and the same feelings surged over him that he had experienced the first time he had heard the exultant thunder of Handel's "Hallelujah Chorus" sweep over him. Ba had once said that he had not the eyes of a ready weeper, but the tears blurred the last words.

Then he opened the door of the little room and went in search of Ba. He did not need to go far. She was sitting on her stool before the fire, her head against the sofa, her hands clasped about her knees. At the first sound of his step she started up, half-smiling, half-frightened, altogether shy. He dropped on his knees and held her until her cheek was against his. Neither of them ever recorded what he told her about the sonnets and his feeling for them. But when she said, "They are for you only. No one else must ever see them," we know his protests.

"They are too great—too universal—to hide under a bushel, my Ba. We cannot do it. I will keep them always, but the ink will fade. I will memorize them, but eventually I will die. No, no, dearest Ba, neither of us has a right to withhold these sonnets."

Still she shook her head, rebelling at the thought of her gift of love being spread across a printed page for all the world to see.

"No, no! I never could publish it under my name, for all the world to point at and say, 'See, this is the way she loves her husband, Robert Browning?' No, Robert, I'll sooner tear and burn them."

But in the end he had his way. They could appear as translations, he said. Everyone knew she did translations from several languages. These could be translations from —oh, Translations from the Portuguese. No one could gainsay her—no one knew Portuguese!

So with more reluctance than her husband could guess, she let the manuscript go to her old-time editor and friend, Mary Russell Mitford, who had a strictly private edition printed, with the imprint "Reading, 1847. Not for Publication."

*B*A had said that Italy was her own especial fairy tale, and it was. But even the gayest and brightest fairy tale has at least one sinister page. While they were still at Pisa the Brownings lived through the first black page of their marriage, the day when a little creature, too small and weak to deal with life, entered and left the world in a matter of hours.

Ba and Robert had lost their first-born.

"We are God's rebellious children, and He leads us where best He can teach us," said Robert.

Later, when they went to Fano, and he saw the famous painting of the Guardian Angel by Guercino in the Church of Sant'Agostino, he gazed so long that other tourists glanced at him curiously and even the monks halted on their rounds and then turned away in quick embarrassment from the stark longing in the Englishman's face. But Browning was unaware of any of them. His whole attention was given to the picture of the tender angel spreading great white wings over the little child he was teaching to pray. Robert's lips moved unconsciously. Perhaps he was framing the lines of one of his loveliest poems:

> Dear and great Angel, wouldst thou only leave
> That child, when thou hast done with him, for me!

The next day he brought Ba with him, and both of them stood silent before the picture. Only by the way they clasped hands to comfort each other did they intimate what it meant to them.

Once Ba would have plunged into an abyss of grief. Now she resolutely turned away from the valley of sorrow. There was Robert to be led back to his natural joyousness.

So far Ba had seen little of Italy except Pisa and, for a few months, the city of Florence. But now she was so flourishing and strong there was no need for them to confine themselves to one spot. So in their second summer in Italy they decided to see Vallombrosa and stay at the famous monastery there. From somewhere Robert got a letter of recommendation to the abbot, and they hurried gaily off to the mountains, having been, as Ba complained, "thoroughly burned out of Florence!"

"We'll avoid the heat and dust—also other people—and start at four o'clock in the morning," Robert decreed. Wilson indulged in a private groan, but Ba was too glad to be starting at all to mind the ungodly hour.

Four o'clock in the morning it was. They reached Pelago, and then boldly attacked their five-mile mountain-climbing trip. Ba, Wilson, Flush, and the luggage were settled in "basket sledges" drawn by four white oxen, while Robert rode on horseback beside them.

To Ba, who had seen few mountains in her life, and who had the capacity to be thrilled to the core, every minute of the five-mile trip (which consumed four hours) was filled with enchantment and awe. She felt exultant and breathless over each glory a new turn in the precarious road brought them.

"It's as though the world is alive with mountains!" she cried out to Robert. "Oh, such mountains, such glory. To think that I never knew such places could be!"

The sun was rising now, and darts of golden light pierced the black ravines to strike the rushing, churning water. Ba caught her breath in ecstasy. "And see the waterfalls, they are transfigured into flowing light. Look to your left, Robert, Wilson."

This rough and agonizingly slow ascent roused no delight in Wilson. She clutched the side of the sledge with so tense a grip that her knuckles ached for hours afterward. She had resolutely kept her fearful gaze on the road above them, but now, in obedience to Ba's command, she ventured to look down the ravine, and promptly screeched.

"Oh, I daren't look, ma'am. I daren't! It is too awful!"

Ba reached over and comforted the frightened maid. "Oh, Wilson, I am so sorry, but it will soon be over. See.

up there you catch a glimpse of something—the monastery, I think." Then she turned and smiled into the understanding, proud eyes of her husband.

The Vallombrosa Monastery was all they had hoped for —clean, cool, peaceful in its setting of mountains and forest and waterfall. But alas, a new abbot was in charge, a rigorously sanctimonious man to whom the sight of a woman was a mortal sin. Robert was welcome enough, but Ba and Wilson couldn't be tolerated. Robert let loose all his charm and persuasiveness, to which most people surrendered, but the abbot only grew more determined. He agreed to let them stay three days, and grudgingly extended it to five, but after that there was nothing to do but recall the sledges and start rolling and slithering down the mountains at three o'clock in the morning. Ba had looked forward to quantities of fresh milk and eggs and butter, but the fare provided at the House of Strangers was fetid bread, oil, and meat.

"The hens must have got themselves to a nunnery," murmured Ba, grimacing as she tried to eat the bread. "This sticks in the throat like Macbeth's amen."

So it was back to Florence for the Brownings. Robert scouted about and discovered a ground floor apartment on the Pitti side of the river, which was spacious and cool, and they were content to settle down in the city with "the Arno's golden arrow shot through her breast" which was to become their real Italian home.

It was in Florence, in March 1849, that they knew one of the most joyous experiences of their lives. Lights had burned in the Browning apartment all night, and at four

o'clock in the morning of March 9th, a weary, feverish
Robert was writing to Henrietta and Arabel to give them
the glorious news that a son had been born to the House of
Browning. "A fine, strong boy with the voice of three!" he
wrote. Ba was doing admirably, and Dr. Harding had
testified that the little creature was the very model of a
beautiful boy! He broke off from sheer excitement, and
Wilson, coming in and seeing his fingers shake as he laid
down his pen, persuaded him to go and lie down.

Lie down? Robert shook his head impatiently. Ridicu-
lous! He wanted to write letters to their families and
friends, proclaiming the wonderful event. Tired? How
could he be tired? He and Ba had a son!

But Wilson had been looking at him with shrewd and
sympathetic eyes. She crossed the room and laid a friendly
hand on his arm.

"You're so beside yourself that you're shaking like a
poplar, sir. And to see you like this would be bound to
distress Mrs. Browning." Crafty Wilson, to strike just the
right note. "Best take a wee rest before you go in to see the
bonny laddie."

Suddenly nature was corroborating Wilson. Her solicitous, kindly face was blurring before his eyes. He pushed
the writing desk aside, took a slow breath, and then reluctantly rose to his feet. No, it wouldn't do to appear before
Ba wearing a haggard face.

"Call me in half an hour, Wilson," he directed. "Or before if Mrs. Browning should desire me." He made his
way to one of the bedrooms and flung himself down on
the bed. Sleep did not come immediately. How could it

with the wonderful fact beating itself over and over on his brain? A son!

From the position of the sun when he waked he knew it must be midmorning. He sat up, startled with a guilty feeling that he might have been wanted and not ready. But Wilson's face, when she put her head around the door, was reassuringly radiant.

"Mrs. Browning wouldn't let you be disturbed, sir, until you'd had your sleep out, but I know she's yearning to see the baby, and she's refused to let the nurse or me bring him to her. That will be for you, she says."

Robert's voice was husky. "My own best Ba!"

He hurried into the airy, sunlit, white-curtained room. The buxom nurse beamed at his approach, and all four of her chins shook. She was a mighty woman, thought Robert, who could easily be cut up into twenty-six Bas! She lifted the little bundle from the cradle and laid it in Robert's arms, shaking with merriment at the awkward way his hands closed around it. For a moment Robert's breath almost stopped, and then, his eyes fastened on the little face, he moved cautiously across the room to the bed. Ba was awake and watching his progress. He thought he had never seen her look so supremely happy or so well. Stooping, he laid the little creature in the waiting curve of her arm, and at that moment the baby opened his mouth in a delicious yawn and wobbled his little fists in air.

"Our son, my precious, dearest Ba! Ours! How great is God's infinite goodness to us."

Ba turned her head to feast her eyes on this miraculous treasure. Then she looked back at the proud face bending over her and smiles and tears came together. "Why—why he is beautiful," she whispered. "I thought Wilson was flattering when she told me so, but so he is! See what a complexion he has managed to get. Occy and Sette, I remember, looked like crumpled red roses. And he has hair! Mrs. Ogilvy's child—"

"Has a six month start," nodded Browning, "and not a hair to his name."

"He has a look of Arabel, I think." Ba continued to explore her son's charms. "Dearest Arabel and Henrietta. How glad they will be. And dear Papa—he will love his grandson, won't he, even if he cannot love me?"

"Who could resist?" her husband said with conviction.

When the baby had been returned to his cradle, Ba asked for Flush. Robert had only to whistle, for Flush had kept an anxious, bewildered vigil outside the door of the white room. Before the summons had died on Robert's lips, the little spaniel was scurrying in. Robert held him so that Ba could whisper to him and he could kiss her hand. "You have a new playmate, Flush," Ba told him. "Show him, Robert."

Flush observed the occupant of the cradle with goggling eyes and gave a distinct sniff. He was still bewildered, but he sensed that a great change was coming over the Browning household and he didn't know whether he considered it good or not.

At one o'clock Robert was rapturously concluding his letter to his sisters-in-law. Dr. Harding had just been there. Ba and the babe were quite wonderfully well. The nurse said he was "so strong—so strong." And the little fingers—why, he had taken hold of his father's nose! The enthralled father had managed to cut off three tufts of hair, rather to the dismay of the nurse—one for the Barrett sisters, one for Treppy, and one for his own mother.

To Ba it seemed more than a miracle that this active, vigorous, lusty-voiced child should be hers. "Such a fat, rosy, lively baby you never saw!" she boasted. And perhaps there was reason for her pride. Wilson reported with glee that experienced nurses cried out when they saw him in his carriage, and the Italian nurse complimented the Brownings by saying he was not like English children, whatever that may have meant!

And then at the very peak of their joy, sorrow struck a bitter blow. Word came from England that Robert Browning's mother was dead, dying just as the joyous news of her grandson's birth reached New Cross. Robert was more than stunned. He was paralyzed with grief. He and his mother had been dearer to each other than anyone ever knew. "Not a day passed without his speaking of her," Ba said.

Ba watched her husband anxiously, with a full heart. He could not eat or write; he deserted his beloved piano. His only comfort was in carrying his son up and down on the terrace; seeing that gave Ba her inspiration.

"We will give our child your dear mother's name," she told him one day. "Only he must carry yours first." So when the baby was three months old, they carried him to the French Evangelical Protestant Church, which was the chapel of the Prussian Legation in Florence. There the mite, sponsored by his parents instead of the usual godparents, was named Robert Wiedeman Barrett Browning. At Ba's wish he was called Wiedeman until he was old enough to talk, when he took things into his own hands by twisting "Wiedeman" into "Penini," whereupon "Penini" he became and remained until it was shortened into the brief "Pen."

Penini must have been a little handful, and between him and Flush the household was no longer placid. At first Flush seemed insanely jealous of Penini, but when he discovered the baby was apparently a fixture, and that "Miss Barrett" and his master were actually fond of him, Flush became the baby's adoring slave.

Penini seemed to have inherited a goodly share of his mother's headlong spirit. He adored soldiers, cannons, and drums, which was a fortunate thing for a baby born in Italy in the middle of the nineteenth century. Every time Robert went for his newspaper, Ba would call after him "Bring me news of a revolution!" and usually he brought her news of two!

She longed to show her little son to her family and friends before he outgrew his babyhood, and there had been talk of going home the summer following Penini's birth, but after Robert's mother's death, Ba said that England looked terrible to Robert, and she would not urge him.

Another reason why the years 1849–1850 did not seem the best time to make the trip home was that in April of 1850 Henrietta had ended five years of wavering and timidity by following Ba's example and marrying her fiancé, Captain Surtees Cook. But Henrietta had found the courage to approach her father and ask his permission. "If you do follow in your sister's miserable footsteps," her father told her bitterly, "I will never allow your name to be mentioned to me again. I have never forgiven your sister. I never will forgive you." He never did.

Henrietta refused to be cheated out of a wedding. She bought a wedding dress and veil, chose Captain Cook's sister as her bridesmaid, and was married publicly by his brother. Ba rejoiced with Henrietta, but she was afraid for Arabel, and Browning reluctantly agreed with her that England was not for them that year. Not that she hoped her father would forgive her, but if she excited his memory about her just now, poor lonely Arabel might reap the repercussions.

But Browning had an impulse to travel. "If we can't go to England, we can go to Rome, Venice, Paris, or even New York."

"Now Robert!" Ba enjoyed teasing him sometimes. "Suppose after we got there I should set my heart on living in New York?"

"Then we should settle there at once. Only please don't set your heart on it, Ba."

They never saw New York, so Ba wasn't tempted, but she did see and entertain many Americans, and admired them greatly. In fact she had a strong liking for America generally because the Americans had a much keener appreciation for Robert's poetry than the English ever had. Her own books were best sellers in the United States, but she was far prouder of the fact that her husband's poetry was sold there—and read. In England her fame far overshadowed his. So much so that when Wordsworth died Elizabeth Barrett Browning was proposed as his successor for poet laureate; no one breathed Robert's name at all. Had they been offered the post jointly, Ba would have been delighted. But England made it plain that she wanted none of Robert Browning, so the post passed to Tennyson.

Both of them published new poems in 1850. Ba offered two volumes called simply *Poems,* the second volume ending with the exquisite sonnets masquerading as *Sonnets from the Portuguese.* Robert's was *Christmas Eve and Easter Day.* The work contained some of his finest poetry, and sold exactly two hundred copies in two weeks. And then all sales seemed to stop dead, while Ba's sales went on and on, which caused her to rage at English stupidity.

But it was the popularity of her books which enabled them really to plan to go home to England in the summer of 1851. They mapped out an ambitious tour. Ba had never seen Venice, so Venice would be first, and then Milan and Switzerland, down the Rhine to Belgium, Paris, and so to England. Even the prospect of escorting a two-year-old baby all over Europe didn't daunt these ardent travelers. Indeed Penini took to traveling like a chip off both blocks! He was fascinated by trains, boats, and carriages—anything that moved—and was enthralled at every new sight.

But Venice, when she saw it, swept everything else out of Ba's mind. She had thought she knew Italy the beautiful, but this—

Standing at the window of the bedroom in their lodging, Ba drew quick breaths of pure rapture. She looked toward the glory of St. Mark's and down at the glimmering canals and knew she could never have guessed anything like this marvel existed.

"It is like stepping into a fairy tale, isn't it, dearest Ba?" Robert put his arm around her and his voice was soft with understanding. "It is like being between heaven and earth," she answered simply. "Never have I touched the skirts of so celestial a place. The beauty of the architecture, the silver trails of water up between all this gorgeous color and carving, the enchanting silence and the moonlight, the music, the gondolas—I mix it all up together!"

How could she ever go away? How did anybody ever go away? But then, alas, came what she couldn't ignore. While she thrived and Penini grew fatter and rosier by the day, the Venetian climate was playing havoc with both Robert and Wilson. Browning grew nervous, unable to eat or sleep, while Wilson dragged herself about her duties feeling half-sick and continually headachy. So Ba was forced to be glad to get away, lamenting, "Alas for these mortal Venices—so exquisite and so bilious!"

Once on their way, however, she couldn't be sorry. Blessed with an inexhaustible fountain of delight over "pleasures new," she thrilled to each new glory along their route. In Milan, when she and Robert went into the cathedral, she astounded and dismayed her husband by announcing she was going to make the climb to the pinnacle.

"The steps are too worn and slippery, Ba," he tried to dissuade her, "I really wouldn't—" But, "Oh, yes you would, and so shall I!" she told him with the gentle impertinence which could be so utterly confounding when Ba chose to use it.

She turned toward the stairs, and with a dubious shrug, Robert followed her, perforce. Up and up and up and up. They went slowly, but in the end Ba mastered the three hundred and fifty steps. While she stood marveling at the awesome snow dream of the Alps, Robert stood and looked at his wife. Could this be the same Ba who had needed every ounce of strength to take a few steps from her sofa to her chair a scant six years ago?

He remembered Mrs. Jameson's remark that Ba was "transformed." Now it seemed to him, standing at the highest point of the cathedral, that she was not so much transformed as transfigured. Truly, they had lived a miracle.

From their beloved Italy they crossed to Switzerland. Ba found the scenery exquisite, but for the pass at Lucerne at first she had no words. They were stopped in her throat. "It is like standing in the presence of God when He is terrible," she said, then, and wept. A thick shawl over her head, she sat out in the open coupé as they passed through great snow walls.

Once again Ba found a place where she would have been content to stay, but Robert urged her on to Paris. They went at full speed, traveling night and day, only stopping for breakfast and dinner. Ba was afraid Penini would be overtired, but when the party reached Paris "he was as fresh as if he had just alighted from the morning star!" He had cried out that the mountains were "due," meaning a great number, and whenever he saw a church he would begin to chant.

Then they came to Paris—Paris, the fascinating, a city which intrigued Ba. It could be so beautiful—and have grinning false teeth dangling from the street corners, wonderful galleries and libraries—and disreputable pictures in the shop windows. Oh, yes, it amused Ba, and she would have liked to stay right there.

If the truth had to be told, she dreaded going to England. When she wrote to Mr. Kenyon, she confessed that she felt quite near enough to England, and that if it were not for Arabel, she wouldn't go. Robert's family had said they would come to the Brownings in Paris, and so might Henrietta Cook and Mr. Kenyon himself. He had promised. *But to give up Arabel is impossible.* She finished her letter sadly:

It's only Robert who is a patriot now, of us two. England, what with the past and present, is a place of bitterness to me, bitter enough to turn all her seas round to wormwood!

Then she dipped her pen again and wrote in a more tender strain. Mr. Kenyon had been a very real fairy godfather to the Brownings. When Edward Barrett tossed his daughter's business affairs aside after her marriage, it was John Kenyon who caught them up and managed them skillfully. And now he had come forward with an endowment for the child, given so delicately that, with all their pride, the Brownings could not refuse.

As she sealed the letter to her cousin she could hear Robert explaining England to his son. "And over in England," he was saying joyously, "there are so many people waiting to love Penini—Aunt Arabel and Aunt Henrietta and Aunt Sarianna, and about a dozen uncles and a dear kind *Nonno*."

Ba's throat contracted at the sound of the Italian word for grandfather. It was Penini's right to know two *nonnos* in England. At last she confessed to herself that the reason behind her clinging to Venice, to snowy Switzerland, and now to Paris, was her ever-present awareness that the nearer she went to London the nearer she would be to Papa. She acknowledged in the depth of her heart that she had no hope he would ever break his word and write or see her again, but they had been so close to each other once that, wherever she was in England, she always would be conscious of his hostile feeling.

She closed her desk and shuddered. For herself she would willingly have remained an exile for life. But—there was Arabel. And Robert. Robert was impatient to see England again. And Penini, yes, he had a right to know his parents' country.

So the Brownings made another channel crossing. It was toward the end of July, but the day was mild, with a gusty east wind and spurts of rain. And the first thing Ba did when she set foot on her native shore once more was to step into a puddle.

*N*OW came the moment when Robert could lead his wife up the box-hedged walk to the door of the modest Browning home in New Cross, and finally present his precious Ba and their wonderful son to his father and sister.

For Ba the trip from London to New Cross had been filled with fears and forebodings. For once she had no pleasure in a journey, no echo of Robert's exuberant delight in the vivid English countryside he hadn't seen for five years. He was going home, thought Ba, but she was about to face the two people who, in all the world, had the best right to be critical of her. Both Mr. Browning and Sarianna had written warm and affectionate letters to her, but now they would see for the first time the wife who had kept Robert an exile in Italy the last years of his mother's life. She had no fears about their loving Penini, but Robert's wife was a different matter. Her smile was hesitant as Sarianna came over the threshold to greet them.

But Sarianna's kiss was far from formal, and a minute later her father-in-law had engulfed Ba's hands in his. Looking up she found his smiling blue eyes were very much like Robert's.

"So this is my second daughter!" How different his gentle, friendly voice was from Papa's brittle one. "I've been waiting for you a long time my dear. Welcome home at last."

All doubt and embarrassment with which Ba had been coping went out in the quick affection of the Brownings' welcome.

As the days went on there was no question that both father and sister had taken Robert's wife and son to their hearts. Ba could truly say, "Most affectionate they are to me, and the babe is adored by Mr. Browning." She did not add, although she probably realized it, that he adored her too. Between Ba and her father-in-law there would grow a very deep and close bond and neither was afraid to show it.

"He's worthy to be my Ba's father," Robert exclaimed, "worthier than her own!"

Of Sarianna Browning, if the truth were confessed, Ba would always stand just a little in awe. Despite a childlike lisp which made her call her brother "Wobert," she was a slightly formidable lady. One of those enviable persons

who always look their best without the least effort and say
and do exactly the right thing at the right moment. She
had a flair for efficiency and executive management of
household and business affairs . "She is very accomplished," observed Ba a bit wistfully, "with a heart to suit
the head."

Invitations and letters of welcome overwhelmed them.
Everyone appeared delighted with the return of the
Brownings. Before they had left Paris Tennyson had
urged them to take over his house, fully staffed (he had
been on his way to Florence), but the travelers preferred
lodgings in Devonshire Street in London, which was near
enough to Wimpole Street to let Arabel run in at least
twice a day. Captain Surtees Cook and Henrietta came
from Somersetshire for a week, and for the first time Ba
and Henrietta had a chance to admire each other's hus-
bands and babies—Henrietta's Altham was less than a
year old. Ba's heart was full when the week was up.

They had other visitors too. The masculine Barretts,
with the exception of Papa, had come to their senses and
one by one arrived at Devonshire Street to marvel at the
new Ba, make friends with Robert Browning, and ex-
claim over their nephew.

Only George was missing. Arabel explained that he was
on a visit in Wales. Robert promptly wrote him, but the
letter was returned twice. And then one September night
a servant appeared with a card bearing an almost illegible
message: *Mr. George Barrett requests the favor of an
interview with Mr. and Mrs. Browning.*

Ba made a choked little sound as her husband read.
Robert raised a quizzical eyebrow.

"Tell Mr. Barrett that we will be honored," he said
dryly. The elderly maid bobbed and retreated. Then Ba
heard a slow, familiar step, and George's spare, austere
figure appeared in the doorway. Ba half started up, but
their visitor turned first to his brother-in-law, who had
risen to greet him.

"Sir"—George was speaking in the solemnly measured
tones which used to amuse Ba so greatly—"Sir, I owe you
an explanation, which I trust you will permit me to offer."
Robert bowed gravely. "I have been on tour in Wales, as
I believe you have heard from my sister, Arabel, and your
letter had natural difficulty in reaching me. When it did,
however, and I had weighed the matter with every consideration, I found myself liking your honorable and
praiseworthy treatment of my sister. Therefore I con-
cluded to come to you and tender my forgiveness for your
rash and secretive actions of five years ago and to proffer
you my friendship."

"So kind of you!" murmured the recipient of these
favors, regarding his brother-in-law with dancing eyes.
Usually it was Robert Browning who was accused of per-
petrating involved phrases. He was enjoying having the
situation reversed!

Now George turned and crossed the room to the sofa
where Ba sat. Her brother surveyed her with a careful
scrutiny and then permitted himself to indulge in a slow
smile.

"Your unorthodox deed has led to beneficial results,

apparently, Ba. Yes, you have benefited amazingly. I am pleased, for I always had an affection for you, although I was in duty bound to express disapproval of your clandestine mode of marriage—"

Ba sprang up and threw her arms around his neck. The meaning of his ponderous words was that he loved her! That was what counted with Ba. He held her close and she whispered so softly that even her husband did not hear, "So I am something more to you than a stone thrown away?"

Now they were all friends. All but Papa. If only Papa would—

But Papa was quite incapable of retreating from a stand once taken. Much against John Kenyon's advice and Robert's better judgment, Ba determined to make one final plea. She wrote her father and persuaded Robert to write as well, begging that if he couldn't forgive her, and had resolved never to see her, would he at least see his grandson?

Then at last Edward Barrett broke his silence. Having proclaimed his resolution never to write to Ba, he ignored *her* letter, but he seized the opportunity to write Robert a blistering reply, enclosing a package containing all the letters Ba had sent him, with their seals unbroken. According to the custom of the time, she had used black-edged envelopes after the death of Robert's mother. For all her father knew, Robert Browning might have left Ba. And he didn't care.

"This is the end." Ba acknowledged her defeat. "I shall never write or hope again."

It was time, the anxious, indignant Robert saw, to hurry her out of England. An unhappy fact was becoming apparent: the health and strength which Ba had found in Italy could be too easily lost in England. Whether it was due to the climate, the constant flurry of entertainments, or Mr. Barrett's savage behavior (or a combination of all three) was anyone's guess. Robert would have rushed her away at once, but Wilson was taking a fortnight's vacation with her family in Sheffield and the Brownings were obliged to wait for her return. Penini was in such a state of bewilderment over her absence that Ba forgot herself a little in caring for him. He refused to let anyone except his mother touch him; she was obliged to sleep with him in her arms; she bathed and dressed him, walked with him, and if she attempted to read or write for more than three minutes at a time, he would cover the page with his hands, saying pathetically, "No more!"

Then Robert had an attack of influenza, and it was the end of September before Ba had the relief of bidding England good-by.

Thomas Carlyle traveled with them to Paris. Both Ba and Robert loved the crotchety old man, and Penini was undaunted by the grim Scot. He probably accepted him as another admirer. One day Ba was hard pressed to strangle her laughter when she heard Carlyle say to her two-year-old baby, "Sir, you have as many ambitions as Napoleon!"

Somewhere between London and Paris Ba lost her cough and forgot her sleepless nights. She was so blooming, in fact, that the Brownings were encouraged to try an apartment in Paris for the winter. Both Ba and the baby adored the city. Penini was charmed by the Punches and the carrousels and the balloons.

The Paris experiment succeeded. Ba was able to entertain her father-in-law and Sarianna, go sight-seeing, and even accept an invitation from George Sand to visit that lady's salon. She considered George Sand one of the great women of the world and felt honored by the invitation. Penini struck up a couple of international friendships, one with the small daughter of the French *concierge,* the other a tiny Russian Princess, both of whom he called boys.

In June Ba put her own desires behind her and turned toward England once more with a smiling face. Since Robert craved a few months in his native land, how could she begrudge him? Besides, it was only in England that the three Barrett sisters could gather together. From June until November the Browning headquarters were at 58 Welbeck Street, close to Arabel, and near enough to Henrietta and her two children, Altham and baby Mary.

Mr. Browning and Sarianna were almost as much at home at 58 Welbeck as Ba and Robert. The old gentleman thought the universe revolved around his grandson. Penini would tag after him hour after hour, begging for the deliciously funny pictures *Nonno* knew how to paint so well.

Penini rivaled the children of the royal family in popularity. Perhaps he was even more of a London sensation. Someone called him an "elf with a scarlet rose-leaf in each cheek." He had a language all his own, a baby muddle of Italian, French, and English, which was de-

lightful, although few people understood more than four
words of what he was saying.

His uncles vied with one another in trying to spoil him,
and the flattered Penini observed he had "such a twantity
of untles." By this time he was old enough and alert
enough to reason that if Papa had a Papa, Mama must
have one too. From scraps of his parents' conversation
and Wilson's observations, he took it into his head that
Mama had done something to displease her papa very
much. One day, apparently absorbed in his paintbox while
Ba and Arabel discussed the hopelessness of the situation,
he suddenly scrambled to his feet and crossed over to his
mother. His eyes were very solemn.

"If you've been very, very naughty, Mama—if you've
broken china, I advise you to go and say, 'Papa, I'll be
dood.' And I'll go with you, Mama. I'm not aflaid of
nossing!"

Ba looked at the child with a sudden wild hope. She
half started up, tempted to follow her son's advice, but
Arabel cried out in such vehement dismay that the moment passed. One wonders what would have happened
had she gone, or if she had sent Penini to Wimpole Street
alone. Would Mr. Barrett have surrendered to the beautiful little chap who combined his mother's delicacy with
his father's vigorous straightforwardness?

On the whole Ba was rather better and enjoyed her stay
in England this year. She and Robert went everywhere—
to Charles Kingsley's home, to Carlyle's, to John Ruskin's
estate, Denmark Hill, to see his collection of Turner's
paintings. Sometimes Robert's glowing accounts of her

comings and goings embarrassed her. "As if," she teased him, "a wife with feet that walk was something of a miracle!"

But again autumn fogs and east winds began to play havoc with her strength, and she was glad when Robert decided it was time to think of Italy. For Ba, Casa Guidi spelled home. Home and strength, security and happiness. In England she would constantly be aware of the shadow of her father's intense bitterness; in Italy, the shadow was like a cloud which occasionally blots out the sun and is gone again. Moreover, even in summer, she confessed she never felt entirely well in England.

"There's always an east wind for me in England," she commented.

In Florence, however, she could enjoy all kinds of activities. She knew and entertained all the prominent English and American residents and visitors in the city, including Harriet Hosmer, the little American sculptress, "who," wrote Ba, "is no taller than a child of twelve." Harriet Beecher Stowe, Dr. and Mrs. Samuel Gridley Howe, and Nathaniel Hawthorne and his family all found a hearty welcome and rich friendship waiting for them in Ba's home.

Ba also took a passionate interest in French and Italian politics and wrote about them abundantly. She called herself a democrat and spoke vigorously for governments which would be in the hands of the people themselves. She had a grandstand view of the *coup d'état* which had made Louis Napoleon, Napoleon the Third, and she witnessed several revolutions in Italy. From her letters it seems she was more thrilled than frightened.

Also she had become absorbed in the study of spiritualism and attended every séance she could. She took a good share of Penini's care upon herself, and of course there was always her poetry.

Yes, Ba had energy enough in Italy!

Meanwhile Penini was growing. Ba declared he had inherited his father's gift for music. This pleased Robert until one day, while he was playing a particularly delicate Chopin étude, he was stopped short by a ferocious din outside the door. Then Penini burst in, followed by Ba. "Oh, Robert," she laughed, wiping her eyes, "how could you stop when Pen has brought three drums to accompany you?"

Robert's face was a study. Then his mouth twitched. "Come here, Pen," he invited. "Papa is going to show you how to play the piano. You must touch the keys with your hands—so—you see?"

Pen saw. He responded to this new pastime with such alacrity that in a few months he was improvising what he called a "beautiful opella."

In the midst of all this Ba found time to write her most ambitious work, a full-length novel in verse. When she was about to begin, she had consulted Hatty Hosmer about the title: Should she call it *Laura* Leigh, or *Aurora* Leigh?

"Oh, Aurora, by all means," said Hatty with prompt decisiveness. "Laura Leigh sounds insipid."

The book itself wasn't insipid by any means. Ba had

long toyed with the idea of writing a full-length novel in verse, and once she began in earnest there was no stopping her. She had plunged into what her American contemporary, Louisa Alcott, called "a vortex." Sometimes Robert Browning protested when he saw her flushed cheeks and heard the excited note in her voice, but she could only beg him, "Don't stop me! This has to come out!"

And, reading the sheets as he gathered them together at the end of each day's work, Robert more than once found himself saying, "Ba, I wish *I* could have written this—it is inspired!"

Elizabeth Browning had always been a rapid worker. Now she wrote as though the verses were being wrung from her. Even Pen stood by to guard her against interruption. Ba was impatient because she had to lay the poem aside for their visit to London in 1855, but the next year she carried it with her, finished it under Mr. Kenyon's roof, and dedicated it to him. And a few days later, when it was safely on its way to the publisher, she left England forever.

"I dare say it will shock you, but you will like a few things, perhaps," Ba told Henrietta, in writing her sister about the poem.

But Ba was totally unprepared for the enthusiasm which greeted the book both in England and America. Three editions sold out in a few months.

Into this novel in verse went all Ba's scorn of rigid Victorian ideas and her fiery conviction that women had a right to be individuals and offer their gifts to the world.

Her characters are as vivid as though she had painted them with colors instead of words and her descriptions are exquisite. The whole book is full of wonderful cadences, fine and vigorous, with strong, singing lines.

Walter Landor said he found "the wild imagination of Shakespeare in it." George Eliot said she and her husband read it three times and that she knew of no book which gave her a deeper sense of communion with a large and beautiful mind. And John Ruskin declared he considered *Aurora Leigh* the greatest poem in the English language.

And so Elizabeth Barrett Browning, who had been virtually a prisoner in the Wimpole Street days, stood at the pinnacle of her success in November of 1856, with everything a woman could hope to have—happiness in her poet-husband and her son; health, as long as she remained in Italy; and fame and fortune from "the greatest poem."

*Y*ES, Ba Browning's life was a joyous one. But sometimes the sharpest pain is an accompaniment to the most perfect delight. Now, when *Aurora Leigh* was being received with such enthusiasm, came the death of the person to whom it was dedicated, John Kenyon. He was the most understanding, steadfast, and generous friend either Ba or Robert Browning ever had.

He had been seriously ill when they were in England, and all three of them had known there could be no hope of another meeting. Ba wrote her beautiful dedication with tears in her eyes and rejoiced that he had lived long enough to hold the book she had given him.

To Ba, especially, his going was a sorrow deeper than

anyone guessed. John Kenyon's hand had been held out to her in her bleakest Wimpole Street days. It was John Kenyon's ivy which had made her windows green, John Kenyon who had carried her first truly ambitious poems to Moxon, the publisher. Above all else, she could never forget his confession that he had maneuvered to bring Elizabeth Barrett and Robert Browning together.

His will proved he had thought of the Brownings to the last, giving both Ba and Robert generous legacies, and perhaps this very fact increased their grief. With his death the tie which had bound her to England seemed to snap.

But eventually Ba's naturally gallant spirit rallied. To be sure, there were shadows across the pattern of her happiness—the separation from her sisters, Papa's terrible unforgiveness, and the fact that for the sake of being well she must keep Robert away from his family.

Then there were some things in which she passionately believed and in which Robert couldn't. She was devoted to spiritualism and Robert was too honest to try to conceal his skepticism. Ba was an ardent admirer of Napoleon III and enthusiastically hailed him as the savior of all Europe. "Pretty slow about it," ejaculated Robert. She had become a vehement Italian patriot, hoping and praying year after year for a united Italy. She lived in a Florence which was humiliated by the presence of Austrian troops of occupation, and hated every minute of it with every ounce of her impetuous spirit.

But taken as a whole, Ba was more supremely happy than she had ever dreamed a woman could be.

Standing at her window one gay February day, watching Florence preparing for the yearly carnival, she heard Pen's running steps and turned to smile at him. Eight years old, he was a graceful, rosy, active child, sensitive and so high-strung that his mother usually had to hold his hands fast to command his attention when he was at lessons.

"Dearest Mama, my sweetest Ba!" He hurled himself upon her in a whirlwind of excitement. "Mayn't I have a blue domino for the carnival. And may I go out into the crowds this year?"

Ba's sound supply of common sense told her the carnival-mad crowds of Florentines were not the most suitable place in the world for a small boy, but it was difficult to resist the entreaty in the sparkling little face. After all, under Wilson's guardianship it would be safe enough to let Pen have his pleasure.

"The domino is altogether possible." She smiled at him reassuringly. "Yes, and a mask. But could I persuade you to go in a black domino?"

Plainly she couldn't. Pen flung himself on the sofa in despair. "It must be blue!" He hated black!

Ba ruffled her son's hair. After all, if it would add to the child's carnival fun, why not? So they agreed—blue domino, blue mask instead of the traditional carnival black.

Wilson—she was now Senora Ferdinando Romagnoli, although Ba and Robert would always call her Wilson, while Pen said Lily—made it for him gladly. Pen protested at first over his parents' stipulation that Wilson must follow him through the crowds, but then his face cleared with his usual swift change of mood.

"Well, Lily, don't call me 'Penini' on the streets! I pray you, don't!"

On the morning of the carnival, Robert watched with fatherly pride the little blue figure whisking down the street, and then put his arms around Ba's waist. "And now we've seen our son off to the carnival, it is high time that Ba thinks of her own domino. Will you have a violet velvet one with a green mask, Ba? Perhaps with pink trimming?" His eyes laughed at her.

"I? But I'm not going—I haven't in years!" Ba cried out in astonishment.

"But you will tonight," argued Robert. "The weather is very bland, you can take no harm. The crowds aren't rough and tumble, only gay. And the ball is a sight worthy of an effort," he coaxed.

Although Robert had taken a box for one of the masked balls and asked some of their Italian friends to share it, it had never entered Ba's head she would accompany him. But now he looked as eager as Pen had when he pleaded for the blue domino.

"There's no time to make me a domino—"

Her husband overrode that objection. She would go out immediately and hire one. Ba caught the carnival fever and did just that. Not violet velvet, however. She contented herself with black silk. And it must be confessed she had a delightful time, enjoying every minute of the ball, mingling with the throng, being saluted, and flashing back gay remarks.

At one o'clock in the morning Wilson's husband served supper in the Browning box. Ba boldly and happily partook of it, going home an hour afterward, tired but buoyant. "And I took no cold!" she reported triumphantly.

In the next four years, however, shadows and sorrows began to crowd close. Mr. Barrett died, as he had lived, with his face still set against both Ba and Henrietta. His will mentioned neither daughter. Long before, Ba had ceased to hope, yet when the tidings came she was numbed. Then word came that Mrs. Jameson, that guardian angel who had come to the rescue of the Brownings fourteen years ago, was gone.

Under the successive shocks her spirits began to sink, her strength was frayed. She wasn't exactly ill, but it was obvious to everyone she had less strength than before John Kenyon's death.

And then one day Robert had letters from England which turned him white and stricken. Finally he summoned the courage to take Ba into his arms and tell her brokenly that Henrietta was dangerously—and hopelessly —ill.

Henrietta, the gay, the strong. Henrietta, to whom happiness had come so late, who had been hounded by poverty, the mother of three little children, all younger than Ba's own Pen.

Ba could neither cry nor speak. She lay in her husband's arms and for a minute he wondered anxiously if she was breathing. Then he saw her lips move and bent his head to catch the faint whisper.

"I never—feared—*that* way!"

She begged Robert to take her to England at once, but he shook his head sadly. It would be too great a strain to see Henrietta suffer. All one could do was pray.

Henrietta's death was the hardest blow to recover from. Shortly afterward the great Italian patriot, Cavour, upon whom all Italy's hopes had been fixed, also died. For Ba it seemed the end of the world. There was no more hope left in the tarnished earth.

It was June, 1861. She was slightly ill, more lassitude than a settled illness, and the weather had turned intolerably hot. Ba sat in her nightgown in the coolest room of the house, languid and very tired. On the twentieth a visitor found her sitting in a doorway in a direct cross draft.

"But the cushion at my back saves me from the draft," Ba replied to her caller's protests.

However, the next day she complained of a sore throat. The worried Robert hastily summoned the doctor, who assured Ba it was only a minor touch of her old trouble and probably would clear up in a few days. But to Robert he confided his suspicions of an ulcer which might develop into something critical. Ba said she felt slightly better and assured her husband that a few days' rest would see her on the mend.

But her sleep was fitful, and when she woke at four o'clock in the morning it was reassuring to find her husband beside her bed. It seemed to her she had never seen him wear a more tender expression. Smiling, she put up her arms and he lifted her from the pillow.

It occurred to her then that never, in all their fifteen years together, had she really told him adequately how greatly she loved him. She had tried to do it in her sonnets, but they had been written before their marriage, and her love had increased and deepened so much during the years. She began telling him now, in words so exquisite that he treasured them in his heart the remainder of his life, although he never could bring himself to repeat them. She told him how much he had meant to her and what he would mean in the years to come. They had done so many marvelous things together, and, please God, they would do so many more.

Robert listened to the small ghost of a voice with a heart full of foreboding. She lay quiet now, her cheek against his.

"You must go to sleep again," he told her, pushing the thick curls back from the high forehead. "Dearest Ba, how do you feel?"

Ba's gallant spirit let her lips curve into a final smile.

"Beautiful!" she said.

And then Ba was gone.

"God took her to Himself," Robert said later, "as you would lift a child from a dark, uneasy bed into the light."

BIBLIOGRAPHY

BENÉT, WILLIAM ROSE, editor, *From Robert and Elizabeth Browning*. John Murray.

BESIER, RUDOLF, *The Barretts of Wimpole Street*. Little, Brown & Co.

BOAZ, LOUISE SHUTZ, *Elizabeth Barrett Browning*. Longmans, Green & Co., Inc.

BROWNING, ELIZABETH, and BROWNING, ROBERT, *The Letters of Robert Browning and Elizabeth Barrett Barrett, 1845–1846*. 2 vols. Harper & Brothers.

HEWLETT, DOROTHY, *Elizabeth Barrett Browning*. Alfred A. Knopf, Inc.

HINKLEY, LAURA L., *Ladies of Literature*. Hastings House Publishers, Inc.

HUXLEY, LEONARD, editor, *Elizabeth Barrett Browning: Letters to her Sister*. John Murray.

KENYON, SIR FREDERIC G., editor, *The Letters of Elizabeth Barrett Browning*. 2 vols. The Macmillan Co.

LENANTON, C., *Miss Barrett's Elopement*. Henry Holt & Co.

WINWAR, FRANCES, *The Immortal Lovers*. Harper & Brothers.

WISE, THOMAS J., editor, *Letters of Robert Browning*. Yale University Press.

Cup 3

DATE DUE			
OCT 1 0 1968		APR 10	
NOV 1 2		OCT 28	
DEC 9		DEC 19	
DEC 12		JAN 2 1	
JAN 6	APR 2		
		FEB 4	
JAN 22		APR 1 4	
FEB 1 1		MAY 7	
FEB 2 6		MAY 29	
MAR 6			
			ALESCO